ITALIAN
LAKES
KNOPF MAPGUIDES

W9-ALB-210

Welcome to the Italian Lakes!

This opening fold-out contains a general map of the region to help you visualize the 6 large geographical areas discussed in this guide, and 4 pages of valuable information, handy tips and useful addresses.

Discover the Italian Lakes through 6 areas and 6 maps:

A Lago d'Orta / Golfo Borromeo
B Lago Maggiore / Centovalli / Val Vigezzo
C Varesotto / Lago di Lugano / Valle d'Intelvi
D Lago di Como
E Bergamo / Lago d'Iseo / Brescia
F Lago di Garda

For each area there is a double page of addresses (restaurants – listed in ascending order of price – cafés, bars, markets and stores), followed by a fold-out map for the relevant area with the essential places to see (indicated on the map by a star ★). These places are by no means all that the region has to offer, but to us they are unmissable. The grid-referencing system (**A** B2) makes it easy for you to pinpoint addresses quickly on the map.

Transportation and hotels around the Italian Lakes
The last fold-out consists of a map of the region and 4 pages of practical information that include a selection of hotels.

Index
Lists all the street names, sites and addresses featured in this guide.

ALPINE EXCURSIONS

Glacial valleys and mountain ranges nearby, soaring to altitudes of over 9,843 feet, provide a playground for sports enthusiasts.

Valtellina (**D** D1)
→ TO, Sondrio Via C. Battisti, 12 Tel. 0342 512500
Lake Como makes a good base for visiting the Bernina mountain range and Mount Stelvio. Val Masino boasts a world-famous climbing center.

Val Camonica (**E** E1)
→ TO, Breno Via Moro
Tel. 0342 512500
The large ski resort at Ponte di Legno is within easy reach of Lake Iseo.

■ Ski resort

ALPINE EXCURSIONS

Very popular with Italians on Sundays.
Rocca / castello: garrisoned fortress / nobleman's fortified residence.
Vaporetto: water bus in the Borromeo Gulf.

DIARY OF EVENTS

April

Ortafiori /
Orta San Giulio (**A** A5)
→ April-May
Tel. 0322 905163
Private gardens open to the public.
International Piano Festival
→ April-June
Tel. 030 43418
Concerts in Bergamo (**E** B3) and Brescia (**E** E4).

May

Mille Miglia / Brescia (**E** E4)
→ Tel. 030 43418
Classic car race.

June

Sagra di San Giovanni
→ June 24
Tel. 0344 57088

Procession of fishing boats on Lake Como between Sala Comacina and Comacina island (**D** B3)
Festival of Ancient Music /
Orta San Giulio (**A** A5)
→ Tel. 0322 905163
Vittoriale degli Italiani Festival / Gardone Riviera (**F** B4)
→ June-Aug
Tel. 0365 296511
Ballets, concerts, theater.

July

Lake Como Festival /
Varenna (**D** C3)
→ First Saturday
Tel. 0341 830367
Carnevale del Sole /
Salò (**F** A4)
→ July-Aug
Tel. 0365 21423
Chariot procession.
Organ Festival / Magadino
→ Tel. 091 7910091
On the Swiss shore of Lake Maggiore (**B** D1).

August

Locarno Film Festival (**B** D1)
→ Tel. 091 7910091

One of the most famous movie festivals in the world.
Corso Fiorito de Verbania Pallanza (**A** D2)
→ First weekend
Tel. 0323 557676
Parade on the passeggiata.
Settimane Musicali (**A** C3)
→ Aug-Sep
Tel. 0323 30150
Chamber music concerts in Stresa and on the Isola Bella.

September

Piano Festival / Orta San Giulio (**A** A5)
→ Tel. 0322 905163
Donizetti Festival /
Bergamo (**E** B3)
→ Tel. 035 399230
The city celebrates the life of the Italian composer, Donizetti (1797–1848).
Exhibition of Naïve Painting in Varenna (**D** C3)
→ Tel. 0341 830367
International exhibition.

October

Antique Fair / Lecco (**D** C5)
→ Tel. 0341 362360

RELIGIOUS ARCHITECTURE

Lombard-Romanesque art
Numerous 11th- and 12th-century buildings characteristically decorated with arcatures (small decorative arcades). **Basilica S. Abbondio** (**D** A2)
Baroque and Counter-Reformation
In the 17th and 18th centuries, this region, which bordered on areas converted during the Reformation, saw the construction of many baroque sanctuaries in a bid to strengthen the Catholic faith. Pilgrimage routes lined with chapels were also built, leading up to sacred mounts. **Sacro Monte di Orta** (**A** A5).

MEDIEVAL CITADELS

The major noble families (Borromeo, Scaliger, Visconti etc.) built castles to protect their lands at strategic vantage points along the lake shores. **Rocca Borromeo** (**B** B5) **Malcesine** (**F** D2)

'VILLE DI DELIZIA' (VILLAS OF DELIGHT)

From the 16th century onward – Villa d'Este in Cernobbio (**D** A5), wealthy Lombard families built magnificent lakeside villas. **Villa del Balbianello** (**D** B3)
The Art of the Garden
The villas are surrounded by superb formal Italian-style gardens (17th–18th century, **Isola Bella**, **A** C3), or English-style landscape gardens (19th century: **Villa Melzi** in Bellagio, **D** B3).

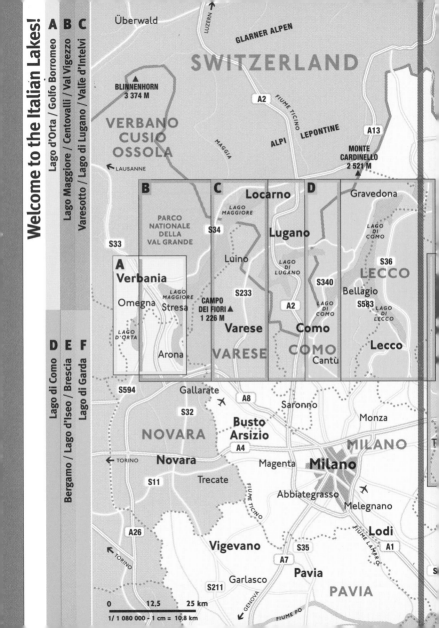

Welcome to the Italian Lakes!

A Lago d'Orta / Golfo Borromeo
B Lago Maggiore / Centovalli / Val Vigezzo
C Varesotto / Lago di Lugano / Valle d'Intelvi
D Lago di Como
E Bergamo / Lago d'Iseo / Brescia
F Lago di Garda

REGION PROFILE

■ The Italian Lake district extends across four regions in Italy (Piedmont, Lombardy, the Veneto and Trentino-Alto-Adige), taking in the Swiss canton of Ticino.
■ These pre-alpine lakes occupy basins created by glaciers during the Quaternary Period (about 1 million years ago).
■ Six major lakes: Orta, Maggiore, Lugano, Como, Iseo and Garda: 373 miles of shoreline.
■ Climate: cold winter (43° F), mild spring and fall (61° F), hot summer (77° F).

LAKE ORTA

TOURIST INFO

Useful abbreviations
ART (*Assessorato Regionale al Turismo*): regional tourist office.
APT (*Azienda di Promozione Turistica*): provincial tourist office.
IAT (*Informazioni Accoglienza Turistica*) or **PL** (*Pro Loco*): local tourist office.
Distretto Turistico dei Laghi (**A** C3)
→ *Via P.pe Tomaso, Stresa Tel. 0323 30416*
The Piedmontese tourist office (Lake Orta and the right shore of Lake Maggiore).
ART Lombardia
→ *Via Sassetti 32, Milan Tel. 02 67561*
The tourist office for the region of Lombardy (the left shore of Lake Maggiore, Lugano, Como, Iseo and the right shore of Lake Garda).

APT Bergamo (**E** B3)
→ *Vicolo Aquila Nera, 2 Tel. 035 242226*
The tourist office for Bergamo, in the *città alta*.
Lugano Turismo (**C** C3)
→ *Piazza Indipendenza, 4 Tel. 091 911 0404*
The tourist office for the region of Lugano.
Comunità del Garda (**F** B4)
→ *Via Roma 8, Gardone Riviera Tel. 0365 290411*
The tourist office for Lake Garda.
Telephone
USA / UK to Italy
→ *011 /00 + 39 (Italy) + city code (including 0) + number*
Calling Ticino (Switzerland)
→ *011 (from USA)/ 00 (from UK) + 41 (Switzerland) + 91 (local dialing code) + number*
Calling abroad from Italy
→ *00 + 1 (USA) / 44 (UK) + number*

To report credit card theft
Visa
→ *Tel. 800 819 014*
AmEx
→ *Tel. 800 872 000*
MasterCard
→ *Tel. 800 870 866*
Useful numbers
Carabinieri (military police)
→ *Tel. 112*
Police and emergency services
→ *Tel. 113*
Vehicle breakdown service
→ *Tel. 116*
Medical emergency
→ *Tel. 118*

WWW.

Useful websites
→ *www.enit.it*
The website of the Italian tourist office.
→ *www.regione. lombardia.it*
The website of the Lombard region.
→ *www.ticino-tourism.ch/*

The website of the Ticino tourist office.
→ *www.parks.it*
Everything you need to know about national parks and other protected areas.
→ *www.perleditalia.it/ perleditalia_laghi.htm*
Listing of the main websites with information about the lakes (tourism, transportation etc.).

GETTING AROUND

Short glossary
Azienda agricola: farm
Città alta / bassa / murata: upper city / lower city / walled city.
Corso: avenue.
Giorno feriale / festivo: weekday / public holiday.
Loc. (località) or *fraz. (frazione)*: abbreviations for a locality.
Lungolago: 'lakeside' promenade.
Passeggiata: promenade following the shoreline.

National park
Regional park

SWITZERLAND

PARCO NAZIONALE DELLO STELVIO

PARCO NAZIONALE DELLA VAL GRANDE

Sondrio

PARCO DELLE OROBIE VALTELLINESI

PARCO NATURALE DELL'ADAMELLO

LAGO DI COMO

LAGO MAGGIORE

PARCO NATURALE DELLA PINETA DI APPIANO GENTILE E TRADATE

PARCO REGIONALE DELLE GRIGNE

PARCO DELLE ALPI OROBICHE BERGAMASCHE

PARCO DELL'ALTO GARDA BRESCIANO

PARCO NATURALE DELLA VALLE DEL LAMBRO

PARCO DEI COLLI DI BERGAMO

LAGO D'IDRO

Bergamo

LAGO D'ISEO

PARCO DELLA GROANE

Novara

PARCO LOMBARDO DELLA VALLE DEL TICINO

Milano

PARCO NATURALE DELL'ADDA

PARCO NATURALE DEL SERIO

Brescia

PARCO NATURALE DELL'OGLIO

LAGO DI GARDA

Lodi

PARCO NATURALE DEL MINCIO

PROTECTD AREAS

(see map on opposite page).

PARCO TORBIERE DEL SEBINO

Situated between the mountains of the Alps and the Po Plain, the Lake district boasts a wide variety of different landscapes.

Alpine mountains
Parco Naz. dello Stelvio

Alcohol
Wines: Valpolicella and Franciacorte (reds) and Lugana (white).
Grappa (Italian brandy).

SHOPPING

All stores in Ticino (Switzerland) accept Euros so you do not need Swiss Francs (CHF).
Gas
Less expensive in Ticino than in France and Italy.
Opening times
Banks
→ Mon-Fri 8.30am–1pm, 2.30–4pm
Stores
Opening times can vary considerably depending on the season.
→ Mon-Sat 9am–noon, 3–7pm. In summer, some shops open late (9–11pm) in tourist centers.
Farm shops
Opening times listed in this book are only a

guideline. It is advisable to phone before you go.

MUSEUMS AND VILLAS

Opening times
→ Summer 9am–6pm. Winter 9am–noon, 2–5pm. Usually closed on Mondays Last ticket sold half an hour before closing. Some sites close in winter.
Price
→ 3 to 7 €. Concessions to students from the European Union.
Unusual museums
Museo dell'Arte del Cappello / Ghiffa (**B** B3)
→ Corso Belvedere, 279 Tel. 0323 59428 April-Oct: Sat-Sun 3.30–5pm. All year round: daily by reservation Hat museum, next to the factory.
Museo dello Spazzacamino / Santa Maria Maggiore (**B** A1)
→ Piazza Risorgimento

Tel. 0324 95091 July-Aug: daily 3.30–6.30pm Chimney sweeps' museum.
Museo della Pipa / Gavirate (**C** A5)
→ Via del Chiostro, 1 to 5 Tel. 0332 743334 April-Oct (by reservation) Pipe museum founded by Alberto Paronelli, a pipe collector.

SIGHTSEEING WITH A DIFFERENCE

By cable car
Many funicular railways afford superb panoramic views over the lakes.
Bidonvia / Laveno (**B** B4)
Spectacular cable car ride.
On skis
View of the shores of Lake Garda from the slopes of the Prada ski resort (**F** C3). There are many other ski resorts in the neighboring mountains (see map on opposite page).

→ Via Roma, 26 Bormio Tel. 0342 901654 Sheer mountains, about 100 glaciers, abundant fauna and flora.
Parco Nazionale della Val Grande (B A2)
→ Villa Remigio Verbania Pallanza Tel. 0323 557960 Densely forested national park, Italy's most extensive area of unspoiled natural beauty. Eagles common.
River valleys
Parco della Valle del Ticino (**B** B6)
→ Via de Amicis Edmondo Lonate Pozzolo Tel. 0331 302260 This park embraces the southern part of Lake Maggiore and the river valley of its effluent, the Ticino.
Parco dell'Adda Nord
→ Via Guglielmo Marconi, 1 Paderno d'Adda Tel. 039 510418 Park in the Adda Valley, effluent of Lake Como.

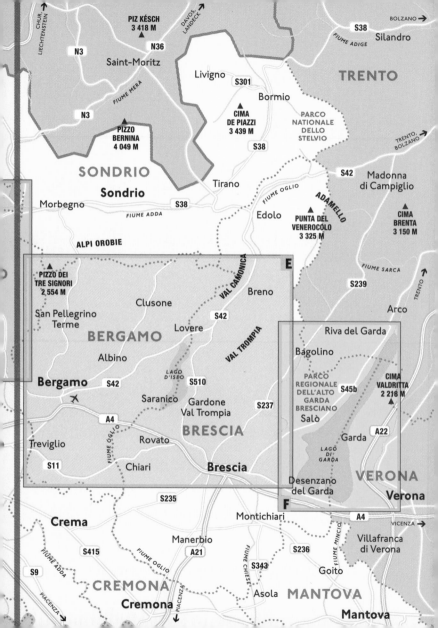

VILLA DELLA PORTA POZZOLO

LAKE MAGGIORE

RIVA DEL GARDA

ARCHITECTURE AND FRESCO PAINTING

The Maestri Comacini
The 'Masters of Como' were renowned architects and sculptors from the Intelvi valley (**C** D3), who were active in European courts between the 14th and 18th centuries. They helped to spread the baroque style outside Italy.

Fresco painting
Mural painting technique which used paint diluted with water and applied to fresh (fresco) plaster. Fresco art reached its pinnacle in Italy between the 16th and 18th centuries, in churches and villas etc.

Antiques market, parade of motorcycles and classic cars etc.

EATING OUT

Opening times
→ noon–2.30pm, 7–10pm
Many restaurants are closed during the winter season.

Osteria, trattoria…
Osteria, grotto, crott: simple food, including open sandwiches and/or a few basic dishes.
Trattoria: small restaurant serving home cooking.
Locanda: inn serving fair-to good-quality food.
Ristorante: gourmet restaurant.

On the menu
Antipasto: starter; servings can be very large: cooked and cured meats, cheese, fish, salads.
Primo: small serving of pasta, risotto or minestrone.
Secondo: meat or fish; side dishes (contorno) are usually ordered separately.
Dolce: dessert.
Two courses – as well as a dessert – are usually enough to satisfy most appetites.

The bill
Bread and cover (pane e coperto) usually account for 2 €. Also allow for mineral water (jugs of water are not usually provided). Most restaurants include a service charge (10%).

À la carte
The prices given in this guide are for an antipasto, a primo or secondo and a dolce, including bread, cover charge and water. Most restaurants do not offer a set menu. The cost of a meal in northern Italy is rarely less than 15 € and usually between 20–25 €. On the Swiss side of the border, prices may be even higher (30 €).

Food in northern Italy
Fairly substantial meals with significant regional variations.

Polenta
The traditional basis of northern Italian food. Thick cornmeal porridge which is served soft or hard.

Olive oil
A staple ingredient, preferably extra virgin. Large-scale production around Lake Garda.

Pasta
Each region has its own recipe for ravioli (casoncelli from Bergamo, strangolapreti from Trentino). And there are thousands of different types of pasta including the lasagnette from Piedmont.

Gnocchi
Little potato dumplings.

Risotto
Dish of rice cooked with meat, fish or vegetable stock. Cep mushroom risotto (risotto ai funghi porcini) is a popular feature on the menu in the Alpine valleys.

Osso-buco
Veal knuckle and marrowbone in a tomato sauce, served with rice.

Cheese and salami
Each valley produces its own salami and cheeses (made from cow's or sheep's milk) which are often served with homemade jam and honey.

Lake fish
Lake fishing is a small-scale industry, so lake fish such as pollan, bleak, pike, perch, sardine and whitefish can be quite expensive.

Pastries
Each city has its local specialty.

Panettone
The most famous cake originated in Milan: a sweet, yeasted fruitcake, originally eaten only at Christmas. There are many regional variations: resta in Como, pandanana in the Veneto etc.

SACRO MONTE DI ORTA

MONTE MOTTARONE

TO: Tourist office

★ **Santuario della Madonna del Sasso** (A A5)
→ *Mon-Sat 9.50–11.50am, 2.50–5.30pm. Mass: Sun 5pm*
The church of the Madonna of the Rock (1748), with its simple façade, is as one with the white granite spur on which it was built. It has an exuberant baroque interior: the nave, transept and cupola are decorated with trompe-l'œil frescos by Lorenzo Peracino. There is a breathtaking panoramic view of the lake from the small square in front of the church.

★ **Orta San Giulio** (A A5)
→ *TO: Via Panoramica Tel. 0322 905163*
Orta San Giulio is a small medieval city with stone roofs. Via Caire Albertoletti is an elegant steep street lined with palaces built in the 15th and 16th centuries by wealthy fishermen. Its crowning glory is the beautiful baroque church of S. Maria Assunta (15th–17th c.). The Piazza Motta is the best vantage point for views of the fresco-covered Palazzo Comunale (1582), the lake and its island.

★ **Isola di Orta San Giulio** (A B5)
→ *Basilica: Tue-Sun 9.30am–12.15pm, 2–6.45pm*
According to legend, this island was guarded by dragons and much feared before the arrival of Saint Julius in 390. He founded the precursor of the basilica, which was rebuilt in the 10th–11th century. The nave has a magnificent black marble pulpit (11th century) carved with the symbols of the evangelists.

★ **Sacro Monte di Orta** (A A5)
→ *Tel. 0322 911960*
A forest path linking the 20 chapels (1591–1770) dedicated to Saint Francis of Assisi runs through the 'Sacro Monte' special nature reserve above Lake Orta. The 376 expressive polychromatic terracotta statues depict important scenes from the saint's life.

★ **Monte Mottarone** (A B3)
→ *Giardino Alpinia, Loc. Alpino April-Oct: Tue-Sun 10am–6pm*
On one side of Mount Mottarone is Lake Orta set in its mountain landscape and, on the other, the sinuous outline of Lake Maggiore. The vast Po Plain stretches away in the distance. Mount Mottarone, with its bare summit (4,890 ft), is one of the *righi d'Italia*, natural 'balconies' dominating the landscape. Further down, the Alpine Garden affords the most spectacular views of the Borromeo Gulf and its string of islands.

A

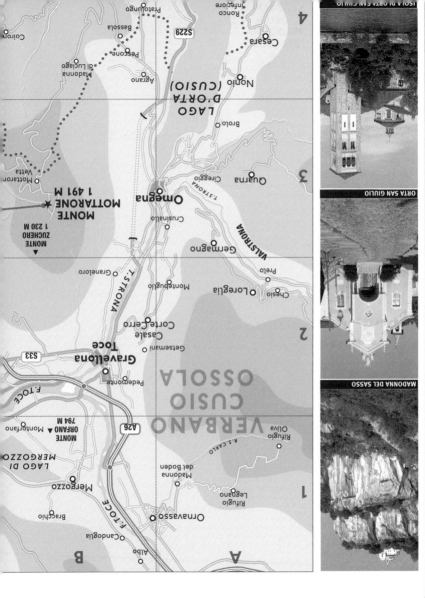

ISOLA DI ORTA SAN GIULIO

ORTA SAN GIULIO

MADONNA DEL SASSO

Lago d'Orta / Golfo Borromeo

From the chapels on the Sacro Monte to the quiet lanes of the island of San Giulio, Lake Orta is a timeless gem. The smallest lake in the region is set in an idyllic landscape of mountains, the most spectacular of which is Mount Mottarone, its slopes wooded with chestnut trees. There is a spectacular view of all six lakes from the summit. In the east, vaporetti sail to and fro across the picturesque Borromeo Gulf, whose four islands – Isola Bella, Isola dei Pescatori, Isola Madre and San Giovanni – bear the stamp of the great Milanese Borromeo family.

RISTORANTE SAN GIULIO   RIFUGIO BAITA C.A.I.

RESTAURANTS

Orta San Giulio (A A5)
Taverna Antica Agnello
→ *Via Olina, 18*
Tel. 0322 90259
Mid-Feb-mid-Dec: Wed-Mon 12.30–2pm, 7.30–9.30pm
The Boschini family, originally from Novara, give pride of place to specialties from their region at the 'Old Lamb'. Excellent lasagnette (lasagne) and rabbit stuffed with olives. Romantic tables on the small vine-covered balcony. À la carte 20 €.
Ristorante San Giulio
→ *Isola San Giulio*
Tel. 0322 90234
June-Sep: daily noon– 2.30pm, 5.30–9pm. Oct-Nov, March-May: Tue-Sun noon–2.30pm, 5.30–9pm
Hidden behind a house with weathered walls, the terrace has been built above the pontoon. Local dishes: tagliolini with cep mushrooms, chestnut gnocchi. À la carte 15 €.
Ristorante Sacro Monte
→ *Riserva Sacro Monte*
Tel. 0322 90220
Feb-Dec: Wed-Mon 12.30– 2pm, 7.30–9pm
A 17th-century stone-roofed house deep in the Sacro Monte wood. You can enjoy beef braised in

Barolo wine or risotto with asparagus. À la carte 20 €.
Mottarone Vetta (A B3)
Rifugio Baita C.A.I.
→ *Tel. 0323 924240*
Wed-Mon noon–2pm, 7.30–9.30pm
With its comprehensive menu, the Italian Alpine Club's chalet will satisfy the largest of appetites. Relax in a deckchair afterwards and embrace the views. Set menu 17 €.
Mergozzo (A B1)
Le Oche di Bracchio
→ *Via Bracchio, 46*
Tel. 0322 80122
Mid-Feb-mid-Jan: Thu-Tue 12.30–2.30pm, 7.30–9.30pm
Roman chef Italo Malchioldi prepares delicious organic cuisine which can be enjoyed overlooking the orchard. Seasonal menu: pea ravioli with basil or hazelnuts, lake fish stewed in wine and honey, fennel gnocchi with black truffles.
À la carte 25 €.
Stresa (A C3)
Piemontese
→ *Via Mazzini, 25*
Tel. 0323 30235
April-Sep: Tue-Sun 12.30– 2.30pm, 7.30–10.30pm. Mid-Feb-March, Oct-Nov: Tue-Sat 12.30–2.30pm, 7.30– 10.30pm; Sun 12.30–2.30pm
The 'Piedmontese' never compromises on quality

AL BOEUC | GIGI BAR | ALISÈI

and the three Bellossi brothers have been preparing classy, creative regional dishes since 1976. Good selection of wines and grappas.
À la carte 30 €.

Isola Superiore dei Pescatori (A C2)
Verbano
→ Via Ugo Ara, 2
Tel. 0323 30408
March-Oct: daily noon–2.30pm, 5.30–9.30pm.
Nov-Dec: Thu-Tue noon–2.30pm, 5.30–9.30pm
At the southern end of the island, Verbano's leafy terrace affords a beautiful panoramic view of the gulf and the vaporetti sailing to and fro. Lake fish take pride of place on the menu: fried bleak, fish ravioli and quenelles.
À la carte 25 €.

Verbania
Pallanza (A D2)
Emiliana
→ Piazza Giovanni XXIII
Tel. 0323 503522 *Thu-Tue 11am–4pm, 6pm–midnight*
Lit by pink neon, Emiliana is always packed. Edo prepares around 50 types of pizza, fresh pasta and homemade desserts.
À la carte 10 €.

Ristorante Milano
→ Corso Zanitello, 2
Tel. 0323 556816 *Feb-Nov: Mon 12.30–2pm; Wed-Sun 12.30–2pm, 7.30–9pm*
While the chef, Edigio, prepares stylish classic cuisine (the lake perch is excellent), his wife, Luciana, looks after diners. You can eat either in the Art Nouveau dining rooms or on the terrace overlooking the port.
À la carte 40 €.

GOURMET PRODUCTS

Local produce
Il Buongustaio /
Orta San Giulio (A A5)
→ Piazza Ragazzoni, 8/10
Tel. 0322 905626
March-Oct: daily 9am–9pm
Wild boar ham, dried fruit loaf from Orta, *toma* cheese from Piedmont, etc.

BARS, PATISSERIES

Orta San Giulio (A A5)
Al Boeuc
→ Via Bersani, 28
Tel. 0322 915854
April-Sep: Wed-Mon 11am–3pm, 6.30pm–2am
Feb-March, Oct-Dec: Wed-Mon 6.30pm–2am
Hidden away in an alley, this is a popular haunt for aficionados of Piedmontese wine. For those who can't drink on an empty stomach Andrea puts slices of mountain salami on the tiny bar for a snack.

Enoteca Re di Coppe
→ Piazza Motta, 32
Tel. 0322 915871
Daily 10am–2am.
Closed Wed in winter
A selection of the best wines, grappas and whiskies, in front of the fire or outside, opposite the Palazzo Comunale.

Mergozzo (A B1)
Birreria Freelance
→ Piazza Cavour, 19
Tel. 0323 80539
Daily 10am–2am (6pm–2am in winter)
Giuliano is fanatical about beer and offers some 120 different varieties, from the excellent Westvleteren to the unusual Corsican Pietra chestnut beer.

Stresa (A C3)
Gigi Bar
→ Corso Italia, 30
Tel. 0323 30225 *Daily 7am–1am. Closed Wed in winter*
A retro-style tea room, decorated in antique pink, the Gigi still sells stylish boxes of *margheritine*, the biscuits made with butter created in honor of Margherita di Savoia's visit to Stresa (1850).

Verbania Pallanza (A D2)
Hosteria Il Cortile
→ Via Albertozzi, 14
Tel. 0323 502816
Thu-Tue 11.30am–3.30pm,
5.30pm–2am
With its patio, vaulted dining rooms and rustic tables, the 'Courtyard' provides a simple setting for a glass of local wine or draft beer and a quick snack (panini, open sandwiches).

SHOPPING

Wood
Dubois / Stresa (**A** C3)
→ Via A.M. Bolongaro, 8
Tel. 0323 32099 *Daily 10.30am–1pm, 3.30–7.30pm (3.30–7.30pm only Nov-Dec)*
In the traditional way, Maurizio carves all the animals in Creation.

Fashion
Alisèi / Stresa (**A** C3)
→ Via Roma, 44
Tel. 0323 934687 *Tue-Sun 9.30am–1pm, 3–7pm*
Silk garments, leather bags and shoes by the Argentinean designer, Eduardo Erretegui.

Fabrics
Penelope /
Orta San Giulio (**A** A5)
→ Piazza Motta, 26
Tel. 0322 905600
Tue-Sun 10am–12.30pm, 2.30–7.30pm. Daily in summer; weekends only in winter
The local tradition of printing floral motifs on the finest Italian fabrics.

→ Map B

ISOLA MADRE

GIARDINI BOTANICI VILLA TARANTO

(Map labels: Solcio, MAGGIORE (VERBANO), Fosseno, Nebbiuno, Tapigliano, Pisano, Colazza, Meina, Ghevio, Dagnente, S33, SAN CARLO BORROMEO, Arona, Ranco, 412 M, Angera, ROCA, Invorio superiore, Invorio inferiore, Oleggio Castello, Paruzzaro, Mercurago, RISERVA NATURALE CANETTO DI DORMELLETTO, A26, S142, Barquedo, Talonno, Dormello, Dormelletto, PARCO REGIONALE LAGONI MERCURAGO, VARA, M)

★ **Stresa** (**A** C3)
→ TO: Piazza Marconi, 16
Tel. 0323 30150
This resort, once popular with the rich and fashionable, has lost none of its period charm. Opulent hotels line the lungolago. At nightfall, elegant couples wander through the narrow streets of the center and drink in the retro-style bars.

★ **Isola Bella** (**A** C3)
→ Palazzo,
Giardino Borromeo
Tel. 0323 30556 March-Sep: daily 9am–5.30pm (5pm Oct)
The most prestigious of the gulf's islands was transformed by the Borromeo family into a baroque ship: it is almost entirely covered by the palace and gardens (1632–71). The 'forecastle' has some incredible grottos lined with mosaics and a gallery decorated with six Flemish tapestries (16th c.) featuring the unicorn, the family's emblem. At the 'stern', there is a series of terraces adorned with statues of angels, gods, goddesses, columns and groves.

★ **Isola Superiore dei Pescatori** (**A** C2)
The picturesque 'Fishermen's Island' has a circular promenade, shaded by chestnut trees, with views of the small port, where fishing boats are moored under the watchful eye of the Madonna erected on the sea wall. Further inland, the 11th-century church of San Vittore is located in a narrow street, behind a leafy garden.

★ **Isola Madre** (**A** C2)
→ Tel. 0323 30556
March-Sep: daily
9am–5.30pm (5pm Oct)
The favorite island of French novelist Gustave Flaubert (1821–80). Visitors approaching by boat will immediately be captivated by the luxuriant vegetation, including North American magnolias, giant bamboos from China and cypress trees from ancient Kashmir. The 16th-century palace houses the Borromeo counts' fine collection of puppet theaters (17th–19th c.).

★ **Giardini Botanici Villa Taranto** (**A** D2)
→ Verbania Pallanza
Tel. 0323 556667
April-Oct: daily
8.30am–7.30pm
The botanical gardens designed by Scotsman, Captain Neil McEacharn (1884–1964), a descendant of the Duke of Taranto, are home to over 20,000 species. Attractions include an avenue of giant coniferous trees, a riot of dahlias and rhododendrons and huge pools covered with waterlilies.

CASTELLI DI CANNERO

CANNOBIO

★ **Rocca Borromeo** (**B** B5)
→ *Angera. Tel. 0331 931300
April-Sep: 9.30am–12.30pm,
2–6pm. Oct: 9.30am–
12.30pm, 2–5pm*
The Borromeo family's
castle (12th–15th c.)
still keeps watch over
the southern part of Lake
Maggiore. Perfectly
preserved with its 12th-
century square tower, this
stronghold has a more
peaceful vocation today as
one of the world's largest
doll museums.

★ **Santa Caterina
del Sasso** (**B** B4)
→ *Leggiuno. Tel. 0332 647172
March: daily 9am–noon,
2–5pm. April-Oct: daily
8.30am–noon, 2.30–6pm
Nov-Feb: Sat-Sun and public
holidays 9am–noon, 2–5pm*
Clinging to a sheer cliff, the
hermitage of Saint
Catherine (12th–17th c.) can
only be reached by boat or
by descending a long flight
of steps. Three open-air
galleries lead to the church,
which houses the tomb
(1195) of the patron saint of
philosophers, and is richly
adorned with blue baroque
frescos.

★ **Statua
di San Carlo** (**B** B6)
→ *Arona Piazza San Carlo
Tel. 0322 249669
Mid-March-Oct: daily 9am–
12.30pm, 2–6.30pm. Nov-mid-
March: Sun 9am–12.30pm,
2–4.45pm*
Monumental statue (1698)
of Charles Borromeo
(1538–84), the most devout
member of this godly family
(*bonromeo*: good pilgrim).
The hollow 75-ft-high
structure glorifies one of the
most fervent champions of
the Counter Reformation.
A steep spiral staircase
leads up to the head. Not
for claustrophobics.

★ **Castelli
di Cannero** (**B** C3)
→ *Cannero Riviera.
Accessible by water taxi
Tel. 0323 788184*
Standing on two islets not
far from the shore, the two
ruined castles at Cannero
Riviera (12th–14th c.) attest
to the legend of the five
Mazzarditi brothers, who
were believed responsible
for a variety of crimes and
thefts in the 14th century.
The Duke of Milan was
forced to mobilize his navy
to flush them out.

★ **Cannobio** (**B** C2)
→ *TO: Viale Veneto, 4
Tel. 0323 71212*
A few miles from the Swiss
border, the last Italian city
enjoys a peaceful existence
behind the intact walls of
its austere medieval
buildings: the Palazzo de la
Ragione, the 13th-century
tower of the Commune

ROCCA BORROMEO

SANTA CATERINA DEL SASSO

Further north along the lakefront guarded by the castles of the Borromeo counts, Lake Maggiore becomes increasingly dwarfed by Alpine peaks. Luxurious villas occasionally afford a glimpse of their magnificent gardens. Just over the Swiss-Italian border lies Ticino, named after the river that feeds the great lake. This canton has lost none of its transalpine atmosphere since its union with Switzerland in 1802. Near Locarno, the Gorges of the Centovalli become a wide valley, Val Vigezzo, on the Italian side of the border. Re, one of the villages in this valley, is the site of a church in Byzantine-Gothic style, which has all the splendor of a cathedral.

SANT'ANNA   MARNIN

RESTAURANTS

Verbania Intra (B B4)
Osteria del Castello
→ *Piazza Castello, 9*
Mon-Sat 12.30–2.30pm,
7.30–10.30pm
Plates of cheese and salami from the Ossolane Valley, mozzarella salad with grapefruit and hunks of black bread, this osteria is all about simple dishes and a family atmosphere, a stone's throw from the lungolago. À la carte 10 €.

Bèe (B B3)
Chi Ghinn
→ *Via Maggiore, 21/23*
Tel. 0323 56326
March-Dec: Wed-Mon
12.30–2pm, 7.30–10.30pm
Adolfo Porta has opened this restaurant in a patrician house in the hillside village of Bèe. First class, creative cuisine – lamb served with peaches and flavored with liquorice – and unobtrusive, attentive service. Sit outside, where you can enjoy a breathtaking view of the lake. À la carte 25 €.

Laveno (B B4)
Il Porticciolo
→ *Via Fortino, 40*
Tel. 0332 667257 Wed-Mon
12.30–2.30pm, 7.30–9.30pm
A haven of peace on the Bay of Laveno, disturbed only by the sound of lapping waters and twittering sparrows. The Porticciolo places the emphasis on the quality and freshness of its produce: pollan with tomatoes and olives, lake fish pâté, carpaccio of bass. À la carte 30 €.

Angera (B B5)
Mignon
→ *Piazza Garibaldi, 22*
Tel. 0331 930141
Daily noon–2pm, 7–11pm.
Closed Tue in winter
Very popular with its numerous regulars, this pizzeria does not vary its menu with the seasons. Thin crusts and lavish toppings keep the discerning customers happy. À la carte 10 €.

Cannobio (B C2)
Sant'Anna
→ *Via Sant'Anna, 30*
Tel. 0323 70682
March-Oct: Tue-Sun
noon–1.45pm, 7–9.45pm
This restaurant is housed in a former presbytery, perched on rocks at the edge of the Sant'Anna ravine. Seated under the ancient chestnut trees, you can feast on river trout and lamb fillet in chestnut honey. À la carte 20 €.

Ronco Sopra Ascona (B C1)
Ristorante della Posta

CANNOBIO MARKET

CANTINA DELL'ORSO

LUINO MAKRET

→ *Via Miseri, 9/11*
Tel. 091 791 8470
Daily 11.30am–2pm,
6.30– 9.30pm.
Closed Wed in winter
The 'Post Office
Restaurant', decked out in
Swiss colors (white tablecloths, red serviettes), is
located at one end of a
lane in Ronco – a village
clinging to the slopes of
Mount Leone. Generous
portions of mushroom
risotto, osso buco... Half
portions (*mezza porzione*)
are available.
À la carte 30 €.

Locarno (B D1)
Il Boccalino
→ *Via della Motta, 7*
Tel. 091 751 9681
Fri-Mon 6.30–10pm;
Tue noon–2pm, 6.30–10pm
Organic, vegetarian
cuisine devised by
Johannes Lanz, a German
chef with a passion for
food. Innovative recipes
and first-class
presentation: tofu salad
with mushrooms, basil ice
cream on a carpaccio of
pineapple with Muscat
grapes. À la carte 25 €.

Al Castagneto
→ *Ponte Brolla*
Tel. 091 796 1419
March-Oct: Thu noon–5pm;
Fri-Tue noon–9pm.
Nov-Dec: Fri-Tue noon–9pm
'The Chestnut Grove', at

the entrance to the Gorges
of Centovalli, serves up
hearty dishes in a leafy
setting. Braised meat
specialties served on old
stone tables. À la carte
20 €.

**Santa Maria
Maggiore (B** A1)
Da Branin
→ *Piazza Risorgimento*
Tel. 0324 94933
Jan-Oct: Thu-Tue noon–
2.30pm, 8–9.30pm
This restaurant has no
printed menu. Speranza
comes to the table and
reels off the simple yet
imaginative dishes of the
day, cooked by her friend,
Giuliàna. Customer
satisfaction guaranteed.
Meal 20 €.

BARS, PATISSERIES

Cannobio (B C2)
Taverna del Torchio
→ *Via Darbedo, 5*
Tel. 0323 739660
Daily 9am–3pm, 6pm–3am
With billiards, karaoke,
a restaurant, three dance
floors and a long bar,
there is never a dull
moment as the 'Winepress
Inn', situated at the foot
of a hill once planted
with vines.

Locarno (B D1)
Marnin
→ *Piazza S. Antonio*

Tel. 091 751 7187
Wed-Fri 7am–7pm;
Sat-Sun 8am–6pm
Watch the world go
by while sampling the
pandanana (Venetian
panettone), the macaroons
made with Kirsch and the
homemade ice cream
prepared by the Venetian
Marnin family.

**Santa Maria
Maggiore (B** A1)
Caffè del Centro
→ *Via Caralli, 12*
Tel. 0324 98019 Daily 7am–
midnight (7.30pm in winter)
A vast selection of coffees
(made with cereals,
liqueurs etc.), teas and
herbal teas is on sale
here. In summer, there
is a massive buffet for
Sunday brunch.

GOURMET PRODUCTS

Traditional market
Cannobio **(B** C2)
→ *Lungolago, Via Magistris*
Sun 8am–2pm
Weekly market for farmers
from neighboring valleys:
ham, cheese, fresh milk...
Ticinese wines
Cantina dell'Orso /
Ascona **(B** D1)
→ *Via Orelli, 8*
Tel. 091 785 8020
Mon-Sat 10am–noon,
2–6.30pm (5pm Sat)

Good selection of wines,
grappas and liqueurs,
made exclusively in the
Swiss canton.

SHOPPING

Art books, lithographs
Alberti /
Verbania Intra **(B** B4)
→ *Corso Garibaldi, 74*
Tel. 0323 402534
Mon-Sat 9am–12.30pm,
3–7.30pm; Sun 4–7pm
There are numerous
lithographs of Lake
Maggiore in the basement.
Libri + Arte / Locarno **(B** D1)
→ *Piazza Stazione*
Tel. 091 743 0333 Mon-Fri
9am–6.30pm; Sat 9am–5pm
Wide range of art books in
the three official Swiss
languages.
Market
Luino **(B** C3)
→ *Lungolago, Via XV Agosto*
Wed 8am–5pm
All kinds of stalls, selling
everything from bikers'
jackets to kitchen utensils
in Luino's busy city center.
Fabrics
Il Telaio di Laura / Santa
Maria Maggiore **(B** A1)
→ *Via Rosmini*
Tel. 0324 94343 Thu-Tue
9–11.30am, 3.30–7.30pm
Signora Guerra weaves
exquisite fabrics and
clothes from natural fibers
(cotton, cashmere).

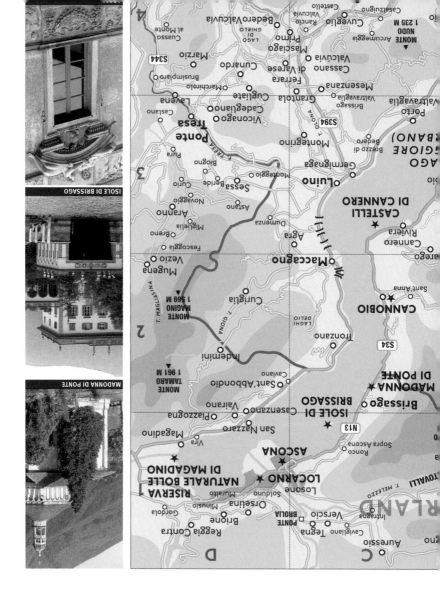

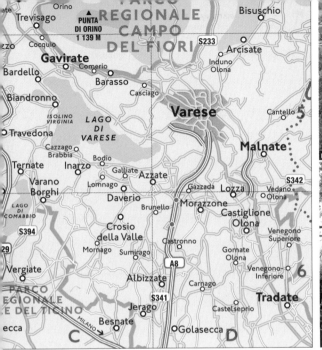

LOCARNO

RISERVA NATURALE
BOLLE DI MAGADINO

and the magnificent Pironi Palace (15th c.), with their red ocher façades.
A century later, Pellegrino Tibaldi, the architect of the Duomo in Milan, designed the cupola of the Santuario della Pietà (1571).

★ Madonna di Ponte (B C2)
→ *Brissago*
Tel. 091 7910091
After passing through Swiss customs, travelers often stop to admire the church of the Madonna of the Bridge (16th c.). Its dome was crowned with an elaborate openwork gallery in Bramantine style by Giovanni Beretta.

★ Isole di Brissago (B C1)
→ *Tel. 091 7914361*
April-Oct: daily 9am–6pm
The wonderful botanical garden on San Pancrazio, the larger of the two Brissago Islands, boasts a fabulous collection of species from all over the world: palm trees from the Canaries, tea plants from China, banana trees from Japan and century plants (Agaves Americanas).

★ Ascona (B D1)
→ *TO: Lungolago G. Motta, 29*
Tel. 091 7910091
Behind the lungolago, which is a popular haunt of wealthy visitors, this resort town boasts many cultural treasures: the baroque façade of the Casa Serodine, decorated with bas-reliefs sculpted by Giovanni Battista Serodine (1620), the choir in the church of St Peter and St Paul (16th c.), adorned with paintings by his brother Giovanni Serodine (17th c.), a pupil of Caravaggio, and the Museum of Modern Art with works by Jawlensky, Klee and Utrillo.

★ Locarno (B D1)
→ *TO: Via Luini, 3*
Tel. 091 7910091
The romantic ruins of the Visconti Castle (14th–15th c.) guard the entrance to old Locarno. There are many churches in the center, each more splendid than the last: Chiesa Nuova (17th c.) with its lavish baroque interior and Sant'Antonio with its red neoclassical façade (17th–19th c.). The hub of the town is the huge Piazza Grande, which is always busy in the early evening.

★ Riserva Naturale Bolle di Magadino (B D1)
→ *Tel. 091 7953115*
The Bolle di Magadino nature reserve in the delta formed by the Ticino River entering Lake Maggiore is home to almost 300 species of birds. There is a pretty wooded path dotted with observation posts.

SACRO MONTE DI VARESE

VILLA DELLA PORTA POZZOLO

★ Chiesa di Santa Maria Fortis Portas (C B6)
→ Castelseprio Parco Archeol.
Via Castelvecchio, 58
Tel. 0331 820438 Feb-Oct:
Tue-Sun 8.30am–7.20pm.
Nov: Tue-Sun 8.30am–7pm.
Dec-Jan: Tue-Sat 8.30am–7pm; Sun 9am–3pm
This church (7th–8th c.), deep in the forest, is virtually all that remains of an ancient city razed to the ground by the Visconti family in 1287. The central apse contains a striking series of Byzantine-style frescos (7th–9th c.) depicting the childhood of Christ: *Annunciation and Visitation*, *Nativity* etc.

★ Castiglione Olona (C B6)
→ TO: Via Roma, 23
Tel. 0331 850084
Castiglione is a red-brick gem, described as a 'little Tuscany in Lombardy': Cardinal Branda Castiglioni (1350–1443) transformed the little town into an ideal Quattrocento city. The collegiate church (1421–8) houses some magnificent frescos by the Florentine painter, Masolino da Panicale (c.1383–1440).

Varese
★ Villa Menafoglio Litta Panza (C B5)
→ Biumo Superiore
Tel. 0332 239669
Tue-Sun 10am–6pm
This 18th-century villa, built on a terrace overlooking Varese and its baroque bell tower (1773), houses art works collected by Count Panza di Biumo: over 2,500 minimalist and conceptual pieces of art. Worth a visit for the fluorescent light installations by the American artist, Dan Flavin.

★ Sacro Monte di Varese (C A5)
→ Via Assunzione, 45
Tel. 0332 229223
This Sacred Way, dedicated to the Mysteries of the Rosary and lined with 14 monumental chapels (17th c.), was designed by Archbishop Charles Borromeo as an instrument of the Counter-Reformation. Walk to the top under the shade of chestnut trees for a breathtaking panorama of the Varesotto.

★ Villa della Porta Pozzolo (C A4)
→ Casalzuigno
Tel. 0332 624136
Tue-Sun 10am–1pm, 2–6pm (5pm winter). Closed in Jan
The art of the Italian garden with its formal landscape design (18th c.): terraces with balustrades and statues of angels, a flight of steps, extended by an avenue of cypresses, climbing to the top of a hill,

C

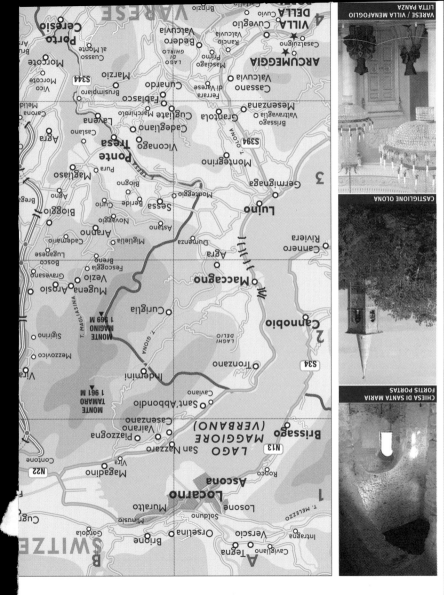
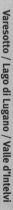

VARESE / VILLA MENAFOGLIO LITTA PANZA

CASTIGLIONE OLONA

CHIESA DI SANTA MARIA FORTIS PORTAS

Varesotto / Lago di Lugano / Valle d'Intelvi

Known as the 'province of the seven lakes', the Varesotto affords unbroken lakeshore views from its footpaths. Varese, its hilltop prefecture, is surrounded by extensive public parks. Villages and villas celebrate the art of fresco painting: walls and façades everywhere are painted with brightly colored motifs. Close to the Italian border in the far south of Switzerland, Monte Generoso dominates the entire Po Plain, and the lake in its foothills is a gateway to the Italian-Swiss 'capital' of Lugano. On the Italian side of the border lies the small Intelvi Valley, which spawned a number of great master builders between the Renaissance and baroque periods.

MONTORFANO   ISOLINO VIRGINIA

RESTAURANTS

Cantello (C B5)
Madonnina
→ L.go Lanfranco da L.
Tel. 0332 417731 Tue-Sun
noon–2.30pm, 7–10pm
A former 18th-century coaching inn on the road to Varese. Seasonal menu – swordfish tartare with lemon, fillet of beef with zucchini flowers – and excellent homemade ice cream. In summer, you can eat in the garden beneath centuries-old beech trees. À la carte 25 €.

Azzate (C A5)
Locanda dei Mai Intees
→ Via Nobile Claudio Riva 2
Tel. 0332 457223
Daily 8–10pm
Cozy inn in a 15th-century villa situated on the town's main square. Traditional cuisine is served in an elegant setting. The sitting room is furnished with period pieces and the dining room has a fireplace and original frescos – ideal for a romantic candlelit dinner. À la carte 25 €.

Varese (C B5)
Montorfano
→Via Santuario, 74
Tel. 0332 227027 Daily
noon–2.30pm, 7.30–9.30pm
At the top of the steep path climbing the Sacro Monte at Varese, the Montorfano is popular with pilgrims and tourists alike. The terrace affords a birds-eye view of the Varesotto. Home cooking. À la carte 10–15 €.

Azzio (C A4)
Terra Libera
→Via Campi Lunghi
Tel. 328 8548333
Sat-Sun noon–2pm, 7pm–midnight. Fri 7pm–midnight. Reserve for lunch
Lasagna with thyme, orecchiette pasta with lavender. A qualified herbalist, Sara creates original vegetarian recipes flavored with homegrown herbs. À la carte 20 €.

Biandronno (C A5)
Isolino Virginia
→ Accessible by boat
Tel. 0332 766268
Feb-Dec: Tue-Sat noon–2pm, 7–10pm; Sun noon–2pm. Reservation necessary
This restaurant is a haven of peace with beautiful views of the tranquil Lake Varese. The chef, Domenico Redondi, the islet's only inhabitant, welcomes customers off the boat. Lombard specialties: perch risotto, pike ravioli. À la carte 20 €.

Viggiù (C B4)
Trattoria Bevera
→ Baraggio di Viggiù
Tel. 0332 486350

FRATELLI GHEZZI   SCHOKO LAND MUSEUM   ANTICHITÀ ORSI

Tue noon–2pm; Wed-Sun noon–2pm, 7–9.30pm Since 1954, the Rizzis have prepared traditional dishes for their regulars. Ducks and chickens are also reared by the family. A local institution. À la carte 10–15 €.

Lugano (C C3)
Osteria La Palma
→ Via Castausio, 3
Tel. 091 923 2422
Mon-Sat 11.30am–2.30pm, 6pm–midnight
A stone's throw from the town center, famous country barbecues (for dinner), on the large turfed terrace: rib steaks, lamb kebabs or tuna fillets cooked to perfection. Barbecue 15 €.

Porlezza (C D3)
Regina
→ Lungolago Matteotti, 11
Tel. 0344 61228 March-Oct: Tue-Sun noon–3pm, 6–9pm
A mouthwatering cheese platter, cakes and pastries attractively displayed, traditional jazz in the background: an appealing Epicurean setting. Traditional cuisine, good staff and a great view over the Bay of Porlezza. Menu of the day 15 €.

San Fedele Intelvi (A D3)
Vittoria
→ Via Provinciale, 116
Tel. 031 830471 Wed-Mon

noon–2pm, 7.30–9.30pm
A mountain atmosphere in the heart of the Intelvi region. Warming minestrone soup, generous servings of risotto and delicious carrot cake prepared by the owner's daughter. À la carte 12 €.

BARS, PATISSERIES

Varese (C B5)
Fratelli Ghezzi
→ Corso Matteotti, 36
Tel. 0332 235179
Tue-Sun 8am–8pm
The oldest patisserie in Varese (1928) is located under the bustling arcades of the Corso Matteotti. Panettones are on display in the window but you can only see the other specialties if you go inside: hazelnut cookies, cotognata (quince jam) with honey, walnut fondant etc.

Bisuschio (C B4)
Playa Colorada
→ Via Gioberti, 14
Tel. 0332 856750 Wed-Sun 6pm–2am (3am Fri-Sat)
Tropical atmosphere, lively young crowd and friendly service. The Colorada bar, on a quiet country road, is famous for its themed evenings: football matches, discos

(Fri-Sat). Long cocktail list.
Lugano (C C3)
Etnic
→ Piazza Maghetti
Tel. 091 923 3825
Tue-Sat 5.30pm–1am
One of the many bars on the square, this is a popular evening haunt for Lugano's younger crowd. Tapas, sangria and cocktails by the pitcher.

GOURMET PRODUCTS

Mushrooms
Ür Fungiatt / Varese (C B5)
→ Corso Matteotti, 49
Tel. 0332 288639
Tue-Sat 9.30am–12.30pm, 3.30–7.30pm
This shop selling 'mushrooms'– in Italian dialect – is heavily stocked from floor to ceiling with jars of ceps and morels, dried or marinated in olive oil. Freshly picked mushrooms are for sale in front of the store.

Swiss chocolate
Schoko Land Museum / Lugano Caslano (C B3)
→ Via Rompada, 36
Tel. 091 611 8856 Mon-Fri 9am–6pm; Sat 9am–5pm
Before buying the Alprose chocolates in the factory store, take a tour round the museum which charts the history of cocoa.

Medicinal and aromatic herbs
Azienda Agricola Terra Libera / Azzio (C A4)
→ Via Campi Lunghi
Tel. 328 8548333 Sat 3pm–1am; Sun 10am–8pm
Lavender, herbal teas etc. The nearby garden is open to the public.

Wine
Enoteca Fiordaliso / Ponte Tresa (C B3)
→ Via Repubblica, 20
Tel. 0332 550111 Tue-Sun 8am–12.30pm, 2–7pm
A stone's throw from the Swiss border, this store sells a wide variety of Italian wines at discount prices.

SHOPPING

Antiques
Antichità Orsi / Varese (C B5)
→ Corso Matteotti, 53
Tel. 0332 234728
Mon 3.30–7.30pm;
Tue-Sat 10am–12.30pm, 3.30–7.30pm
Gilded frames, statues, chandeliers, vases etc.

Fashion
Fox Town / Mendrisio (Switzerland) (C C4)
→ Via A. Maspoli, 18
Tel. 848 828888
Daily 11am–7pm
All the major Italian labels at rock-bottom prices.

VILLA CICOGNA MOZZONI

ARCUMEGGIA

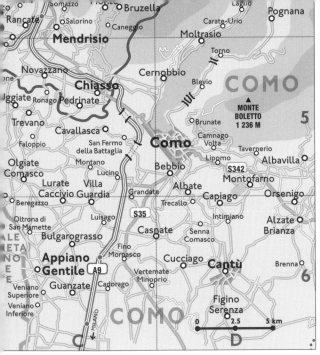

LUGANO

VALLE D'INTELVI

and side paths leading to the chapels. Inside the villa (16th–17th c.), the art of fresco painting reaches its pinnacle: there are frescos on walls, ceilings and doors.

★ **Arcumeggia** (C A4)
The walls of this remote village are covered with mural paintings. Artists like Usellini, Montanari and Brancaccio were inspired in the late 1950s by a wide variety of themes such as faith, everyday life, sport and nature.

★ **Villa Cicogna Mozzoni** (C B4)
→ Bisuschio Piazza Cicogna
Tel. 0332 471134
April-Oct: Sun and public hols
9.30am–noon, 2.30–7pm
This is a rare example of a Renaissance villa (15th–16th c.). A porch leads to the arcaded courtyard with its pink paving stones, fountains and an English-style landscape garden. This villa is a riot of color: from the external walls, decorated with portraits of noblemen and women, to the fireplace lintels and painted coffered ceilings.

★ **Monte Generoso** (C C4)
→ Accessible by train from the Capolago station
Tel. 091 6481105
This rack railway train runs slowly between the station at Capolago and Mount

Generoso, 4,593 feet above. After climbing for 40 minutes, there are spectacular views of the Alps, the Po Plain and the Apennines.

★ **Lugano** (C C3)
→ TO: Riva Albertolli
Tel. 091 9133232
The city of Lugano sits at the back of a picturesque bay surrounded by mountains. Its main cultural attractions are on the lakefront: the Romanesque church of Santa Maria- degli-Angioli (15th c.), adorned with fine frescos by Bernardino Luini (16th c.), and the romantic municipal park, its plane trees trailing their branches

in the water.

★ **Valle d'Intelvi** (C D3)
→ Tel. 031 831217
The villages in the Intelvi Valley rival each other in elegance with their lavishly decorated churches. This area produced the *Maestri Comacini*, craftsmen renowned in the European courts (14th–18th c.). Laino is a must with the church of San Lorenzo containing sculptures by Barberini (1667) and the chapel of San Giuseppe, adorned with a fresco by Quaglio (1717). Scaria is also worth seeing for the church of Santa Maria, a baroque masterpiece.

VILLA CARLOTTA

VILLA DEL BALBIANELLO

★ Bellagio (D B3)
→ *TO: Piazza della Chiesa, 14*
Tel. 031 950204

Bellagio stands on the headland where Lake Como branches into three (the name comes from *bi lacus*, or 'between the lakes'). Made famous by the French novelist Stendhal, this very attractive town has a promenade lined with oleanders, terraces sheltered by weathered multicolored awnings and steep stepped lanes. The Villa Serbelloni (18th c.) is situated at the highest point of the town. Spectacular views from the garden planted with fragrant roses and orange trees.

Como
A small, very pretty town.

★ Duomo (D B1)
→ *Piazza del Duomo*
Daily 7am–noon, 3-7pm

Como's cathedral, a masterpiece by the *Maestri Comacini* (14th–18th c.), is a harmonious blend of Gothic and Renaissance styles: lacy stonework, pink and white marble façade and the so-called Porta della Rana (door of the frog), carved with fantastic figures (Rodari brothers, 1509). Inside, beneath the ornate blue and gold vaulted ceiling, the aisles are hung with sumptuous Flemish and Italian tapestries (16th–17th c.).

★ Basilica
S. Abbondio (D A2)
→ *Via Regina Teodolinda, 35*
Tel. 031 269563
Daily 8am–6pm

A perfect example of Lombard Romanesque style with its two square towers and arcatures, this basilica was consecrated by Pope Urbino II in 1095 and dedicated to the patron saint of the city. Thanks to its impeccable restoration (19th c.), it has escaped the ravages of time; the apse's Byzantine frescos (1300) are vibrant once more.

★ Villa Carlotta (D B3)
→ *Tremezzo. Tel. 0344 40405*
March-Oct: daily 9am–11.30am, 2–4.30pm.

April-Sep: daily 9am–6pm

This villa (17th c.), named after one of its last residents, Princess Charlotte of Prussia (1831–55), has a monumental staircase leading down to the lake. The spacious drawing rooms contain various expressive sculptures by Canova (1757–1822, *Maddelena, Palamede*). The English-style landscape garden (19th c.) features varieties of azaleas and rhododendrons.

★ Villa del Balbianello (D B3)
→ *Lenno. Tel. 0344 56110*
April-Oct: Tue, Thu-Sun 10am–noon, 3.30-6.30pm

The spectacular gardens of the Villa del Balbianello

D

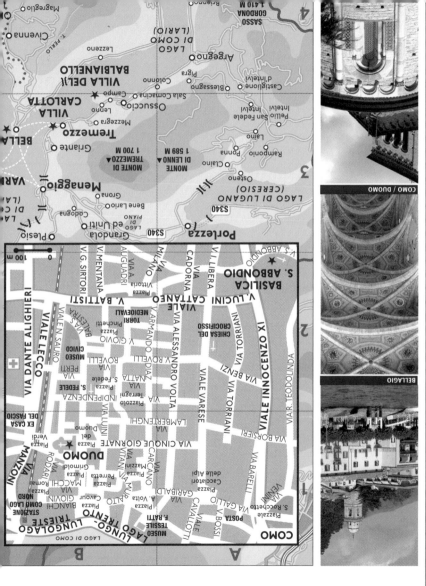

Lago di Como

COMO / DUOMO

BELLAGIO

Only pedestrians and cyclists can explore the monuments and streets at the center of the *città murata* (walled city) of Como. From the waterfront Piazza Cavour, with its restaurant terraces, the lake begins winding its way between the sheer slopes of the bare-topped mountains, reaching its full width at Bellagio. The relatively unspoiled region of the Alto Lario (the northern part of the lake) still has many Romanesque churches and palaces. The shores of the lake are dotted with *ville di delizia* (villas of delight) – a source of inspiration for some of the world's greatest artists: Liszt (the 'Dante' symphony), Stendhal (*The Charterhouse of Parma*) and Rossini (*Tancredi*).

LOCANDA DEL DOLCE BASILICO   PASTICCERIA MONTI

RESTAURANTS

Como
Il Solito Posto (D A1)
→ *Via Lambertenghi, 9*
Tel. 031 271352 Tue-Sun
noon–3pm, 7–10.30pm
The 'Usual Place' for people living in Como has not let its standards drop since 1888: the tables are stylishly laid, the service is impeccable and the cuisine inventive – asparagus pâté, swordfish with rosemary and cheese platter with homemade jam. À la carte 25 €.
Navedona (D A5)
→ *Via Pannilani*
Tel. 031 308080 Wed-Mon
noon–2pm, 7–9pm
This restaurant's dining rooms are filled with the fragrance of dozens of flower arrangements. Nestling in the small valley of Cosia, the Navedona places the emphasis on the harmony of flavors: escalope of pan-fried pork in Malvasia wine with apples, saffron risotto with zucchini flowers. À la carte 40 €.
Brunate (D A5)
Locanda del Dolce Basilico
→ *Mulatteria per San Maurizio, 24. Tel. 031 221003*
Mon-Tue, Thu-Sat 8–9.30pm;
Sun noon–2pm, 8–9.30pm.
Reservation necessary

The proprietor named his inn 'Sweet Basil' in homage to his native Liguria, where this plant is renowned for its fragrant bouquet. The cuisine is Mediterranean with a twist: zucchini fritters, gnocchi with basil and garlic. Terrace planted with lime trees. À la carte 15–20 €.
Cernobbio (D A5)
Della Torre
→ *Piazza Vittorio Emanuele, 3. Tel. 031 511308*
Daily noon–2pm, 7–10.30pm (midnight for pizza)
Perfectly placed for gazing down on Como and its magnificent Duomo. Perched above the village of Cernobbio, the restaurant aims to satisfy all appetites: the chefs prepare risotto and beef carpaccio to order and bake delicious pizzas in the wood-burning stove. À la carte 15 €.
Campo di Lenno (D B3)
Trattoria del Grifo
→ *Via Mattia del Riccio, 19*
Tel. 0344 55161
July-Aug: daily noon–2pm, 7.30–9pm. Sep-June: Thu-Tue noon–2pm, 7.30–9pm
Signora Bianchi cooks traditional recipes for her regulars: excellent gnocchi *burro e salvia* (butter and sage dumplings) and fluffy polenta served with pork.

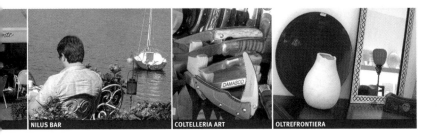

NILUS BAR   COLTELLERIA ART   OLTREFRONTIERA

À la carte 10 €.

Tremezzo (D B3)
Al Veluu

→ *Via Rogaro, 11*
Tel. 0344 40510 March-Oct:
Wed 7.15– 9.30pm; Thu-Mon
12.15– 2.15pm, 7.15-9.30pm
Comfortably seated at
a table in the garden
planted with olive trees,
you can enjoy the view of
the Riviera of the Azaleas
while sampling the
delicious southern Italian
cuisine: the restaurant's
own antipasto with figs,
pollan with olives and
more. À la carte 25 €.

Crandola
Valsassina (D C3)
Da Gigi

→ *Piazza IV Novembre, 4*
Tel. 0341 840124
July-Aug: daily noon-2pm,
7.30–9pm. Sep-June: Thu-Tue
noon-2pm, 7.30-9pm
Named after their late
father, the restaurant run
by the three Gobbi sisters
is a credit to the family.
When in season, the
wonderful cep mushrooms
picked in the valley are a
treat. Excellent platter of
mountain cheeses. À la
carte 25 €.

Perledo (D C3)
Crott del Pepott

→ *Loc. Vezio*
July-Sep: daily 10am-10pm.
May-June, Oct: Sat-Sun
10am-10pm

In the kitchen of this
former mill, built
overlooking a ravine,
Maria tends the fire where
meat, fish and polenta are
still cooked on stone.
Panini made with the
day's leftovers are always
available. Meal 10 €.

PATISSERIES, BARS, ICE CREAM PARLORS

Erba (D B5)
Gelateria Sartori

→ *Via Volta, 8*
Tel. 031 611819
Tue-Sun 8am-10pm
Signor Sartori's creamy
homemade ice cream is
a great favorite. Iced fruit
tarts, granita and great
espresso.

Como
Pasticceria Monti (D B1)

→ *Piazza Cavour, 21*
Tel. 031 301165
Wed-Mon 7am–midnight
One of the busiest terraces
in Como, opposite the
lake. Never short of *resta*
– Como's almond cake–
the hundred-year-old
patisserie owned by the
Monti family also has a list
of some 15 different types
of coffee to tempt (or
torment) the indecisive.
Caffè Novecento (D B2)

→ *Viale Lecco, 23*
Tel. 031 266228
Daily 7am-10pm

The counter is laden with
mouthwatering snacks to
accompany your aperitif
and the bar serves fresh
fruit cocktails.

Varenna (D C3)
Nilus Bar

→ *Via Riva Garibaldi, 1*
Tel. 0341 815228
April-June: Wed-Mon 10am–
1.30am. July-Aug: daily
10am-1.30am
The ideal place for
watching Varenna's pretty
old port: ducks and swans
on the shore, fishermen
sailing into the center of
the lake and children
hurtling down the sloping
alleyways. Refreshing
affogati – drinks topped
with a scoop of ice cream.

GOURMET PRODUCTS

Liqueurs
Distilleria di Liquori /
S. Maria di Piona (D C2)

→ *Abbazia di Piona*
Tel. 0341 940331 Daily
9.20am-noon, 2.30-5pm
The monks sell herb
liqueurs made to secret
recipes at the abbey gate.
Their beneficial properties
are shown on the
packaging so you can
decide whether you need a
pick-me-up or something
to aid digestion cure or
rheumatism.

Yogurts
Azienda Agricola Piero
Butti / Vendrogno (D C3)

→ *Via Biagini, 4*
Tel. 0341 870246
Yogurt fresh from the farm,
natural or packed with fruit
such as cherry, raspberry,
and apricot, as well as dog
rose or elderberry.

SHOPPING

Knives
Coltelleria Art /
Premana (D C3)

→ *Via Roma, 6/a*
Tel. 0341 890432
Tue-Sun 9am–noon,
2.30-7.30pm
Famous knives from
Premana, made by 200
craftsmen in the Varrone
Valley.

Home design
Oltrefrontiera /
Como (D B1)

→ *Via Muralto, 18/20*
Tel. 031 269256
Mon 3-7pm; Tue-Sat
10am-1pm, 3-7pm
Furniture and decorative
objets from Africa and Asia.

Fashion
Mantero / Como (D A2)

→ *Via S. Abbondio, 8*
Tel. 031 321510
Mon-Fri 2-6pm
Fashion house founded in
Como in 1902. Wonderful
embroidered fabrics:
clothes, scarves and ties.

LECCO

SAN PIETRO AL MONTE

(18th c.), at the end of a small peninsula, transform a barren, rocky site into a garden of Eden. At the highest point of the promontory stands a lovely yellow ocher loggia with plants twining round its columns.

★ Gravedona (D C1)
→ TO: Via Molo Vecchio, 45
Tel. 0344 89637
This tranquil little city in the Alto Lario has a long history of rebellion against signorial rule. Near the beach is the church of Santa Maria del Tiglio with an elegant, finely carved bell tower (11th–12th c.). The Palazzo Gallio (16th c.), a fortified villa designed by

Pellegrino Tibaldi, still stands guard on the outskirts of the city.

★ Abbazia di S. Maria di Piona (D C2)
→ Colico Tel. 0341 940331
Daily 8am–12.30pm, 2–7pm
This Cistercian abbey (12th c.) is in an isolated position on a promontory. It is still home to about ten monks who tend the vegetable garden and orchard behind the cloister, which has capitals carved with plant motifs (13th c.).

★ Varenna (D C3)
→ TO: Piazza Venini, 1
Tel. 0341 830367
This is a very pretty medieval village curled round its old port. A

walkway suspended above the water runs alongside houses and cliffs. Castello Vezio (14th c.) commands the most unbroken view of Lake Como. The gardens of the Villa Monastero (16th c.) on the road to Lecco are full of cypresses.

★ Lecco (D C5)
→ TO: Via Sauro Nazario, 6
Tel. 0341 362360
This industrial city's main claim to fame is as the birthplace of Alessandro Manzoni (1785–1873). The renowned Italian writer set his famous novel, I Promessi Sposi (The Betrothed, 1824–7), in Lecco and his statue can be found in its largest square.

The family villa has been converted into a literary museum.

★ San Pietro al Monte (D C5)
→ Accessible by foot
Tel. 0341 551576 Sun and public hols 9am–noon, 1.30–4pm (and by arrangement)
It takes an hour to walk up the steep path to the basilica of St Peter's on the Mount (10th–11th c.), 1,312 feet above the town of Civate. After several centuries of neglect, San Pietro was rediscovered in 1930 with its decoration intact, including a lavishly worked baldacchino (1070) combining frescos and stucco work.

MONTE ISOLA

RISERVA NATURALE REGIONALE TORBIERE DEL SEBINO

Bergamo

★ Pinacoteca dell' Accademia Carrara (E E1)

→ *Piazza Carrara 82/a Tel. 035 399643 April-Sep: Tue-Sun 10am–1pm, 3–6.45pm. Oct-March: Tue-Sun 9.30am–1pm, 2.30–5.45pm*

Bergamo's art gallery, founded in 1796, displays paintings by the Bergamasque, Venetian and Lombard schools between the 15th and 19th centuries. There are some particularly fine works by Pisanello (*Leonello d'Este*, 1440), Bellini (*Madonna and Child*, c.1480), Raphael (*San Sebastiano*, 1501) and Lotto (*Portrait of Lucina Brembati*, 1523).

★ Basilica Santa Maria Maggiore (E C1)

→ *Piazza Duomo Mon-Sat 9am–12.30pm, 2.30–6pm (5pm winter); Sun 9am–1pm, 3–6pm (5pm winter)*

Polychromatic red marble lions (1353) guard the porch of the basilica (12th–17th c.) that faces onto Piazza Vecchia. The interior, remodeled in the Renaissance and the 18th century, contains a Flemish tapestry of the Crucifixion (1698), inlaid choir stalls executed by Capoferri (1533) and a confessional in exuberant baroque style (1704).

★ Capella Colleoni (E C1)

→ *Piazza Duomo April-Sep: daily 9am–12.30pm, 2–5.30pm. Oct-March: Tue-Sun 9am–12.30pm, 2–5.30pm*

The ornate funerary chapel (1476) of Condottiere Colleoni (1400–75) was erected, according to his wishes, on the site of the basilica's sacristy, which was simply demolished. A gilded equestrian statue glorifying the wealthy soldier of fortune stands on top of the sarcophagus.

★ Chiesa di Santa Maria delle Neve (E D2)

→ *Pisogne Via Romanino, 18 Tue-Sun 9.30–11.30am, 3–6pm*

The church of Our Lady of the Snow (15th c.) contains a fresco cycle (1532–34) by Romanino (1484–1559) depicting the Passion. It is remarkable for its highly detailed treatment – in the style of Bosch – and its realistic characters with intense expressions.

★ Parco Nazionale delle Incisioni Rupestri (E F1)

→ *Capo di Ponte Loc. Naquane Tel. 0364 42140 Tue-Sun 8.30am–7.30pm (5pm winter)*

This national park, founded after the discovery of the rock engravings in 1955, boasts thousands of figures etched onto some 100 rocks. Bronze-age pictures (around 2000 BC) can be told apart from the more realist Iron-age engravings (around 1000 BC) because

E

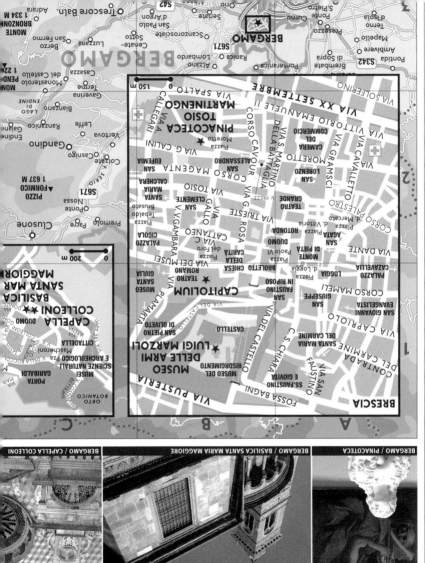

BERGAMO / CAPPELLA COLLEONI

BERGAMO / BASILICA SANTA MARIA MAGGIORE

BERGAMO / PINACOTECA

There are two Bergamos: the medieval and Renaissance *città alta* (upper city), with its harmonious ensemble of stone buildings, and the more modern *città bassa* (lower city), sprawling over the plain at the foot of the hill. Brescia, its rival, boasts an impressive hilltop castle and an art gallery filled with paintings by local and national artists. With Bergamo on one side and Brescia on the other, Lake Iseo provides the setting for another gem: the island of Monte Isola. Further upstream, the Val Camonica preserves ancient rock engravings, works of art from another time.

TRATTORIA DEI CACCIATORI   RISTORANTE DELLA CORONA

RESTAURANTS

Bergamo
Cooperativa
Città Alta (E C1)
→ *Vicolo Santa Agata, 19*
Tel. 035 215741
Mon-Tue, Thu-Fri 8.30am–3am; Wed 11am–3am; Sat-Sun 9am–3am
This cooperative eatery is popular with customers on tight budgets, particularly students. Simple food, basic decor and always busy. À la carte 10 €.

Trattoria del Teatro (E C1)
→ *Piazza Mascheroni, 3/a*
Tel. 035 238862
Tue-Sun noon–3pm, 7.30pm–midnight
Although the trattoria ceased to be part of the 'Social Theater' in 1982, it has kept both its name and its clientele of culture lovers. Typical Bergamasque cuisine: snails in parsley (order in advance), braised kid and rabbit, meltingly soft polenta. À la carte 25 €.

Ol Gopì e la Margì (E B3)
→ *Via Borgo Palazzo, 27*
Tel. 035 242366 Tue-Sat noon–3.30pm, 7.30pm–midnight; Sun noon–3.30pm. Closed in Aug
Gopì and Margì are the two Commedia dell'Arte characters from Bergamo. This restaurant places the

emphasis on tradition and local products: *casoncelli* (typical Bergamasque ravioli dish) with sage leaves, black truffle risotto. Set menu 37 €.

Ponteranica (E B3)
Trattoria dei Cacciatori
→ *Via Croce dei Morti, 20*
Tel. 035 571195
Mon, Wed-Fri 7–9pm; Sat-Sun noon–2pm, 7–9pm
The 'Huntsmen's Trattoria' is located at an altitude of 2,461 feet. Polenta is cooked in a huge pot over the fire by the door while, behind the bar, Signor and Signora Barachetti prepare family recipes: during the hunting season, rabbit is macerated in wine for two days. À la carte 10–15 €.

Sale Marasino (E D3)
Ristorante della Corona
→ *Via Roma, 7*
Tel. 030 9867153
Wed-Mon 7.30pm–1am
The 'Crown' is a classy restaurant housed in a fine 14th-century building. Vaulted dining rooms decorated with period fireplaces and garlands of hydrangeas set the scene for delicious meals made with homegrown vegetables. À la carte 25 €.

Monte Isola (E D3)
Ristorante Milano
→ *Loc. Peschiera*
Tel. 030 9886134

PASTICCERIA CAVOUR · RETIFICIO ARCHETTI PAOLO · SCURI RAFFAELE

March-Jan: Tue-Sun noon–2pm, 7pm–1am
This small fish restaurant on the passeggiata serves a superb array of antipasti: lagoon trout, dried sardines (an island specialty) and rolled perch, etc. À la carte 15 €.

Iseo (**E** D3)

La Cantina
→ *Viale Repubblica, 6/a*
Tel. 030 9822041 Tue-Fri, Sun 10.30am– 2.30pm, 7–11pm; Sat 7–11pm
The 'Cellar' is an institution dating back to the 17th century. It has an extensive selection of Franciacorta wines. Plates of cheese and cooked and cured meats, grilled lake sardines. The chatty owner, Andrea, is from Sardinia. À la carte 20 €.

Mompiano (**E** E4)

Castello Malvezzi
→ *Via Colle S. Giuseppe, 1*
Tel. 030 2004224 Wed-Sun 12.30–2pm, 8–10pm
In the midst of a wooded estate, the Malvezzi Castle (16th–17th c.) overlooks Brescia. A modern cuisine – lightly marinated tuna tartare, black risotto with gorgonzola and green celery – is served in the baroque dining rooms. Extensive wine list.
À la carte 35 €.

Brescia

La Grotta (**E** B2)
→ *Vicolo del Prezzemolo, 10*
Tel. 03044068 Thu-Tue 11am–2am. Closed in Aug
Valley cheese, locally-made salami and Brescian bacon: this old inn, at the end of a no-through road, uses products sourced throughout the region. This is an authentic eatery whose decor (walls painted with rural scenes) is incredibly kitsch. À la carte 15 €.

ICE CREAM PARLORS PATISSERIES, BARS

Bergamo

Bar Accademia (**E** D1)
→ *Via S. Tomaso, 74*
Tel. 035 220523 Mon 5pm–2am; Tue-Sun 11.30am–2am (3am Fri-Sat)
Berliner Hans Breuer serves typically German drinks and dishes: draught beer, sausages, Tyrolean gnocchi. After a few drinks regulars often sing along to the Bavarian music.

Vineria Cozzi (**E** C1)
→ *Via B. Colleoni, 22*
Tel. 035 238836 Sat-Thu 10.30am–2am (Thu-Tue 10.30am–2am in winter)
An old wine bar in the Upper City (1848) which serves excellent cheeses and wines.

Pasticceria Cavour (**E** C1)
→ *Via Gombito, 7/a*
Tel. 035 243418 Mon-Sat 7.30am–midnight; Sun 8am–midnight
Bergamo's delicious *polenta e osei* (little cakes made with hazelnut cream and almond paste) make a colorful window display in the city's oldest pâtisserie (1850).

Brescia

Gelateria del Biondo (**E** A2)
→ *Via Vittorio Emanuele II, 115 Tel. 030 41031 Daily 8am–midnight (Thu-Tue 8am–11pm in winter)*
Brescias most famous ice cream parlor, offering a wide range of flavors, including cinnamon, green apple, violet etc.

SHOPPING

Wooden boats

Cantiere Nautico Montisola/ Monte Isola (**E** D3)
→ *Via Peschiera M., 1*
Tel. 030 9886219
Traditional boat-building is still a flourishing industry on the island.

Wrought iron

Scuri Raffaele/ Bergamo (**E** D1)
→ *Piazza Mercato del F., 4/a*
Tel. 035 247010
The Scuri family of wrought iron craftsmen still use the century-old workshop and traditional iron beating techniques.

Fishing nets

Retificio Archetti Paolo / Monte Isola (**E** D3)
→ *Loc. Peschiera Tel. 030 9886270*
Paolo continues the tradition of making nets, which are used both by fishermen and for making hammocks.

Glassware

Monzio Compagnoni Gianromano / Bergamo (**E** D1)
→ *Piazza Mercato del F., 10*
Tel. 035 226492
Gianromano's glassware studio: wall lamps decorated with Commedia dell'Arte characters, trays, plates, lampshades etc.

GOURMET PRODUCTS

Franciacorta wine

Fratelli Berlucchi / Borgonato di Cortefranca (**E** D3)
→ *Via Broletto, 2*
Tel. 030 984451 Mon-Fri 8.30am–noon, 1.30–5pm. Wine tasting by reservation
The five Berlucchi brothers are renowned for their *spumante* (sparkling wines, champagne method).

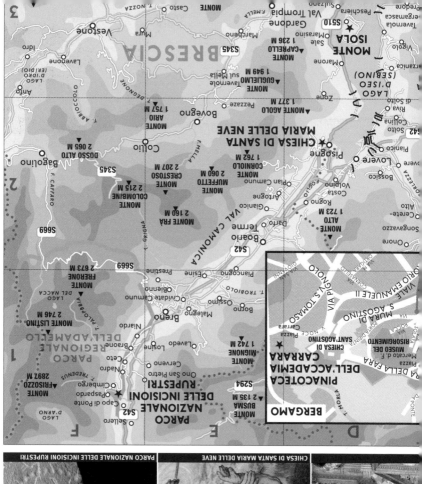

PARCO NAZIONALE DELLE INCISIONI RUPESTRI

CHIESA DI SANTA MARIA DELLE NEVE

Map labels (top map):

TORBIERE DEL SEBINO · Olseo · Provaglio d'Iseo · Monticelli Brusati · Brione · Sarezzo · MONTE PREALBA 1 271 M · Agnosine · Odolo · Sabbio-Chiese · 1 136 M · Vobarno · F.CHIESE

Monticelli Brusati · Ome · Villa-Carcina · MONTE PREDOSA 1 077 M · T. GARZA · Roè-Volciano · Berniga · Sopraponte

gonato di te Franca · Passirano · Saiano · Gussago · Concesio · Caino · S237 · Fostaga · Villanuova sul Clisi

Cazzago an Martino · Rodengo-Saiano · Collebeato · Bovezzo · Nave · MONTE UCIA 1 169 M · Gavardo

Castegnato · Cellatica · Mompiano · Serle · Paitone · Muscoline

Ospitaletto · Botticino-Mattina · Nuvolento · Prevalle · Calvagese della Riviera

Travagliato · Roncadelle · Torbole · A4 · BRESCIA · Nuvolera · S45b · F.CHIESE · Macesina

Berlingo · Casaglia · Castel Mella · Volta · Rezzato · Mazzano · 0 · 3.5 · 7 km

Lograto · S235 · San Zeno Naviglio · S11 · VERONA

D · E · F · 4

BRESCIA / MUSEO DELLE ARMI LUIGI MARZOLI   BRESCIA / CAPITOLIUM   BRESCIA / PINACOTECA

they appear more symbolist in style.

★ **Monte Isola** (**E** D3)
→ TO: Peschiera
Tel. 030 9825088
Describing itself as the largest inhabited lake island in Europe, Monte Isola has preserved traditional activities such as boat-building, net-making and sardine-drying. Cars are not allowed on the island, so you can explore the passeggiata that runs alongside the fields of olive trees by bicycle.

★ **Riserva Naturale Regionale Torbiere del Sebino** (**E** D3)
→ *Iseo*
Tel. 030 9823141

Mined for fossil fuel since the 18th century, the peat bogs of the Sebino have been a listed nature reserve since 1983. Pools filled with waterlilies are a fisherman's paradise (eel, pike, carp, perch). A pretty raised walkway winds its way through the pools, affording a perfect vantage point for admiring this area of natural beauty.

Brescia
★ **Museo delle Armi Luigi Marzoli** (**E** B1)
→ *Via Castello, 9*
Tel. 030 293292 June-Sep: Tue-Sun 10am–5pm. Oct-May: 9.30am–1pm, 2.30–5pm
This museum of weaponry, founded in 1988, is housed

in the keep of the Visconti Castle (14th c.). Nearly 600 pieces, dating from between the 15th and 18th centuries, attest to the key role played by Brescia in the arms industry. There are many firearms in the collection, made by renowned craftsmen such as Cominazzo. The panoramic view over the city is an added bonus.

★ **Capitolium** (**E** B1)
→ *Piazza del Foro*
Tel. 030 59003 Site closed, but the temple can be visited
The Roman temple (AD 74), built by order of Emperor Vespasianus (AD 9–79), was partially rebuilt in the mid-20th century. A few

surviving Corinthian columns stand out against the blue of the sky.

★ **Pinacoteca Tosio Martinengo** (**E** B2)
→ *Piazza Moretto, 4*
Tel. 030 3774999 June-Sep: Tue-Sun 10am–5pm. Oct-May: 9.30am–1pm, 2.30–5pm
Brescia's art museum is housed in a Renaissance palace shaded by tall cedars. It has hundreds of works, including some particularly interesting 15th–16th-century paintings by Brescian artists: *Madonna and Child* by Foppa (c.1427–c.1515), *San Girolamo* by Romanino and *Cena in Emmaus*, a masterpiece by Moretto (1498–1554).

PUNTA SAN VIGILIO

MALCESINE

0   2.5   5 km

A   **B**

★ Sirmione (F B5)
→ TO: Viale Marconi, 2
Tel. 030 916222
Nestling between the
two shores of the narrow
peninsula, this former
fishing village is famous
for its hot spring (156° F):
thousands of people come
every year to take the
waters at the thermal spa.
Sirmione was also one of
the fiefs held by the Della
Scalla (Scaliger) family, who
ruled the region in the 13th
and 14th centuries, before
the Viscontis took over.
Virtually surrounded by
water, the Scaliger Castle
with its crenellated towers
(13th c.) guards the only

entrance into the city. The
lake views are magnificent.
★ Grotte di Catullo
→ Piazzale Orti Manara
Tel. 030 916157 Tue-Sun
8.30am–7pm (5pm winter)
The windswept tip of this
promontory is the site of the
ruins of the largest Roman
villa in northern Italy (1st
century BC– AD 1st century),
long regarded as the home
of the Latin poet Catullus
(c.87–c.54 BC). Long
arcades, an immense
terrace and Roman bath
complex.
★ Peschiera
del Garda (F C6)
→ TO: Piazza Betteloni, 15
Tel. 045 7550381

The red brick fortifications
of this military town,
erected by the Republic of
Venice in the 16th century,
are still intact, although
overgrown with vegetation.
The monumental gates –
the Verona Gate (1553) in
the west and the Brescia
Gate (1558) in the east –
lead into the heart of the
town: an incredible maze
of streets formed by two
islands linked by a single
bridge, one home to the
civilian population and the
other the garrison.
★ Punta
San Vigilio (F C4)
→ Garda. Tel. 045 7255884
There are spectacular views

of Lake Garda from
peaceful, leafy San Vigil's
Point. At the end of an
ancient path lined with
cypress trees, a gnarled
olive dating from the
11th century points the
way down a cobbled lane
leading directly to the
small port.
★ Malcesine (F D2)
→ TO: Via Capitanato, 6
Tel. 045 7400044
Perched on a rocky spur
overlooking the lake, the
Scaliger Castle and its
unusual pentagonal keep
(13th–14th c.) dominate the
village of Malcesine, with its
narrow winding lanes. The
fortress is now devoted to

F

GROTTE DI CATULLO

SIRMIONE

4
Berniga

Gazzane — Roè-
Volciano
Vobarno

GARDONE RIVIERA
Salò
VITTORIALE DEGLI ITALIANI
Toscolano-Maderno

F. CHIESE

Mornaga
Navazzo — Zuino
Formaga
Sasso

MONTE PIZZOCOLO ▲ 1 582 M
MONTE ALBERELLI ▼ 1 167 M
MONTE ZINGLA ▼ 1 497 M
MONTE GALLO ▲ 1 136 M

3

LAGO DI VALVESTINO
MONTE CARZEN ▼ 1 508 M
Mignone
Costa

MONTE DENERVO ▲ 1 450 M
MON
SA

BRESCIA

Lavenone — **Idro**

PARCO REGIONALE DELL'ALTO C BRESCIA
Cadria
Magasa
Moerna
Vio Zumie Vio

LAGO D'IDRO (ERIDIO)
Anfo
ROCCA D'ANFO

2

Bondone
CIMA SPESSA ▲ 1 820 M
Lodrone Ponte Caffaro

Bagolino

F. CAFFARO

Condino
Storo
MONTE STIGOLO ▲ 1 699 M
F. CHIESE

S240
S237
S669

B
A
1

Lake Garda – the largest lake in Italy – stretches between the Po Plain and the Alps. The southern end has a Mediterranean feel, its hills thickly planted with olive trees and vines. In summer, when the far shore is shrouded in mist, you could be taking a dip in the Mediterranean: near Salò, the shoreline forms a series of crystalline bays. By contrast, the northern end of the lake is bordered by sheer mountains. The wind tears through this natural corridor, making the lake a paradise for the windsurfers who can be seen skimming tirelessly between the two shores.

RISTORANTE BAR OSVALDO   CAFFÈ GRANDE ITALIA

RESTAURANTS

Desenzano del Garda (F A6)
Al Portico
→ *Via Anelli, 44*
Tel. 030 9141319 Wed-Mon noon–3pm, 7–11pm (plus Tue 7–11pm in March-Sep)
First-class, simply dressed fish: whitefish with herbs, bass in an aromatic stock, turbot with olives. Good selection of white Lugana wines. À la carte 25 €.

Sirmione (F B5)
Il Guelfo
→ *Via Bisse, 1*
Tel. 030 9905923 Thu-Tue noon–2am (5pm–2am in winter)
Dine on the terrace under the jujube tree in the magical glow of the torches and castle lights: stuffed bread cooked in wood-ash, platters of cheese, cooked and cured meats, pasta... Inside, bottles of the region's vintages are on display. À la carte 10–15 €.

Sant'Ambrogio di Valpolicella (F D5)
Groto de Corgnan
→ *Via Corgnan, 41*
Tel. 045 7731372 Mon-Sat 8–10pm. Reservation necessary
Giorgio Soave spends the day carefully preparing the mouthwatering dishes that you will have for dinner. You will also find on the wine list a perfect accompaniment for the Venetian antipasti or tagliatelli with mushrooms. À la carte 45 €.

Garda (F C5)
Graspo
→ *Piazzetta Calderini, 12*
Tel. 045 7256046 Feb-Nov: Wed-Fri 6.30– 9.30pm; Sat-Sun noon–2pm, 6.30–9.30pm. Reservation essential at the weekend
Choose between fish and meat, and then from a variety of Venetian specialties including *sarde in saor* (sardines). The entire Brangian family helps prepare the dishes that change daily. Set menu 30 €.

Locanda San Vigilio
→ *Punta San Vigilio*
Tel. 045 7255884 Daily noon–1pm, 8–10pm
This elegant inn is housed in a 16th-century villa at the tip of Saint Vigil's Point, with a wonderful view of the lake. Sea-bream, spaghetti with crab and olives. À la carte 40 €.

Malcesine (F D2)
Lido Paina
→ *Loc. Paina*
Tel. 045 7400587 Daily noon–2.30pm, 6.30– 10pm (closed Mon mid-Sep- mid-Oct)

PANE E SALAME   RAIMONDI   OLÉ !

This beachside restaurant serves tasty dishes to the sound of lapping waves. Pizzas, *caserecci* pasta in a fish sauce, gnocchi with gorgonzola and hazelnuts. À la carte 15 €.

Riva del Garda (F D1)
Ristorante Alpino
→ *Via Cerere, 10*
Tel. 0464 552245
Daily 11am–3pm, 7–10pm (closed Sun in winter)
The 'Alpine', on a small square in the labyrinthine streets of the old city, is very popular with locals. Rustic decor (gingham tablecloths, wooden terrace) and hearty Trentino cuisine: polenta with goulash, *strangolapreti burro e salvia* (spinach ravioli in a sage and butter dressing). À la carte 15 €.

San Felice del Benaco (F A4)
Ristorante Bar Osvaldo
→ *Loc. Porto Portese*
Tel. 0365 62108
Daily noon–2pm, 7–9pm (closed Tue from July-Sep)
Diners can enjoy the restaurant's *antipasto completo* (prawns, smoked salmon, mussels, sardines, etc.) and the grilled fish (eel, bass, octopus, sole etc.) gazing over the turquoise waters of Salò bay. À la carte 20 €.

ICE CREAM PARLORS, BARS

Sirmione (F B5)
Caffè Grande Italia
→ *Piazza Carducci, 24*
Tel. 030 916006
July-Aug: daily 8.30am–2am. Oct-mid-Nov, March-June: Tue-Sun 8.30am–2am
The hundred-year-old café on the prettiest square in Sirmione boasts a clientele that has included some of the greatest figures in 20th-century history: Pirandello, Churchill, etc. Delicious fruity cocktails and homemade cakes.

Peschiera del Garda (F C6)
Bar Gelateria Centrale
→ *Via Dante, 4*
Tel. 045 7550327 June-Sep: daily 8.30am–1am. March-May, Oct-Nov: Thu-Tue 8.30am–1pm, 3–8.30pm
This former artillery barracks (19th c.) has been converted into a bar with a spectacular floating terrace. Wonderful alcohol-flavored ice creams (gin, vodka, Grand Marnier...).

Riva del Garda (F D1)
Pane e Salame
→ *Via Maroco, 22*
Tel. 0464 541954
Tue-Sun 10am–1am
A chunk of bread (*pane*) and a couple of slices of *salami.* All you need to complete the picture is a glass of wine from Trentino or the Veneto.

Limone sul Garda (F D2)
Bar Gelateria Al Porto
→ *Via Porto, 24*
Tel. 0365 954116
Daily 8am–midnight (Sat-Thu only in April, Oct-Nov)
This ice cream parlor with its attractive terrace is near the jetty away from the hustle and bustle of the town. Beer, wine, cakes and homemade ice-cream.

GOURMET PRODUCTS

Charcuterie
Macceleria Vivaldelli /
Riva del Garda (F D1)
→ *Piazza della Chiesa, loc. Varone*
Tel. 0464 522057 Tue-Fri 8am–12.30pm, 3–5pm; Sat-Mon 8am–12.30pm
This butcher is famous for *carne salata,* beef salted for 20 days, a Trentino specialty.

Olive oil
Comincioli / Puegnago del Garda (F A4)
→ *Via Roma, 10*
Tel. 0365 651141
Daily 9am–7.30pm
Produced entirely under vacuum by the Comincioli family, this oil preserves all the goodness and flavor of the fruit.

Lugana wine
Provenza / Desenzano del Garda (F A6)
→ *Via dei Colli Storici*
Tel. 030 9910006 Mon-Sat 8.30am–noon, 2.30–6.30pm
Sample whites and the full-bodied red *negresco* under the porch of the winery.

Vin de Valpolicella
Raimondi / Gargagnago (F D5)
→ *Via Monte Leone, 12*
Tel. 045 7704974
Lucia, a Colombian, continues to run the small 17-acre vineyard founded in 1989 with her late husband, an Italian American. She specializes in light reds.

SHOPPING

Art books
Merigo Art Books / Manerba del Garda (F B5)
→ *Via dei Colli, 4*
Tel. 0365 551832
Open by request
Bookstore specializing in the decorative arts and exhibition catalogues.

Fashion
Olé ! / Bardolino (F C5)
→ *Via Borgo Garibaldi, 7*
Tel. 045 6210991 March-Oct: daily 10am–1pm, 4.30–9pm
Brightly colored, sexy womenswear. In summer, the store sells its own bags and straw hats.

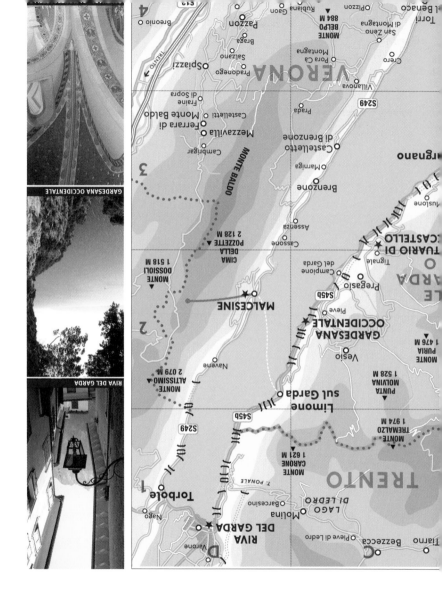

GARDONE RIVIERA

VITTORIALE DEGLI ITALIANI

art and knowledge: library, dining room containing mementos of Goethe's travels through the region, and a natural history museum. A cablecar climbs the slopes of Mount Baldo to an altitude of 5,742 feet.

★ **Riva del Garda (F** D1)
→ *TO: Viale V. Clementino, 14 Tel. 0464 554444*
The picturesque town of Riva, with its majestic backdrop of mountain peaks, is the best-known lake resort in the Trentino region. It is worth a visit for its colorful buildings, baroque architecture and *rocca* (castle) surrounded by a moat.

★ **Gardesana Occidentale (F** C2)
The mountain slopes sometimes sweep all the way down to the water's edge along the west shore of Lake Garda. As a result, the road along this problematic section of the lake, opened in 1931, has 70 tunnels and 56 bridges. The upper section of the cliff road commands dizzying views.

★ **Santuario di Montecastello (F** C3)
→ *Tignale Tel. 0365 73019 March-Oct: daily 9am–6pm*
This sanctuary (14th c.), perched on the edge of a sheer cliff, over 2,297 feet

high and dedicated to the Madonna, affords more incredible panoramic views. The choir has a fresco of the *Coronation of Mary* in the tradition of Giotto. Early risers will hear the bells chiming when the church opens its doors.

★ **Gardone Riviera (F** B4)
→ *TO: Corso d. Repubblica, 8 Tel. 0365 20347*
Wealthy travelers head for the tall towers of the luxury hotels in the most fashionable resort on Lake Garda. The passeggiata is a riot of scents and colors: magnolias, bay trees, palms, rose bushes, lemon trees and wisteria.

★ **Vittoriale degli Italiani**
→ *Tel. 0365 296511 April-Sep: Tue-Sun 8.30am– 8pm (9am–5pm Oct-March)*
The last home of Italian writer Gabriele D'Annunzio (1863–1938) who occupied the villa from 1921 until his death. The 22-acre estate, rather grandly named 'Monument to Italian Victories', boasts among other things a submarine, the prow of a battleship (spoils of war presented by Mussolini) and the artist's vast mausoleum. You can take a fascinating guided tour of rooms packed with books, objects and works of art.

FERRY ON LAKE MAGGIORE

Cambiasca (B B3)
Agriturismo Campagnoli
→ *Via in Lunga, 7*
Tel. 0323 559122
These four comfortable
apartments, run by the
Comero family of
stockbreeders, are near the
entrance to the Val Grande
National Park. Acclaimed
restaurant in the proprietors'
residence. From 60 €.
Cannobio (B C2)
Albergo Alessandra
→ *Via Nazionale, 77*
Tel. 0323 70278
Signora Minoggio's small
guesthouse (8 rooms) is a
stone's throw from the
Swiss border. Breakfast on
the terrace overlooking the
lake. Chinese restaurant on
the first floor. From 65 €.
Locarno (B D1)
Pensione Olanda
→ *Via ai Monti, 139/a*
Tel. 091 751 4727 March-Nov
Signora Balbina provides a
warm welcome to regulars
and new guests alike. This

ten-room guesthouse has
a delightful flower-filled
terrace above Locarno.
Reservation recommended.
From 45 €.

C VARESOTTO /
LAGO DI LUGANO /
VALLE D'INTELVI

Cantello (C B5)
Madonnina
→ *Largo Lanfreanco, 1*
Tel. 0332 417731 Feb-Dec
This former coaching inn
(18th century) has 14 rooms
decorated in style: terracotta
tiled floor, period furniture
etc. From 106 €.
Cunardo (C B4)
**Agriturismo della Tenuta
del Maglio**
→ *Via del Maglio, 15*
Tel. 0332 716439
Six rustic rooms with lovely
views of meadows owned by
the Valagussa family. Take
this opportunity to sample
their wonderful ostrich meat
and eggs. From 62 €.

Marchirolo (C B3)
Drive Hotel Pegaso
→ *Strada Statale 233, 27*
Tel. 0332 997140
The 'Pegasus' is a luxury
motel of 35 rooms built on
the site of a former riding
school. It has a private
parking lot, small garden,
swimming pool, tennis
court and picnic tables
with a view over the valley.
From 78 €.
Orino (C A4)
Agriturismo I Marroni
→ *Loc. Gaggiolo, 1*
Tel. 0332 631308
Two well-equipped
apartments in a stone
house in a landscape
of raspberry canes and
chestnut trees tended
by Signor De Bernardi,
a former Milanese
industrialist. Behind the
house a footpath leads
to the Campo dei Fiori
Regional Park. From 80 €,
without breakfast
(minimum stay two nights).

BY TRAIN

Trains are inexpensive
and there are regular links
from Milan.
www.trenitalia.it
Milan-Lakes
Usually depart from
Milano Centrale (or Milano
Porta Garibaldi)
→ *Toward Brescia (45 mins)
and Lake Garda (approx.
1 hr)*
→ *Toward Como (1h) and
Lugano (approx. 1 hr)*
→ *Toward Varese
(approx. 1h)*
→ *Toward Lake Maggiore ,
to Stresa (approx. 1 hr)*

BY CAR

Speed limits
→ *50 km/h (31 mph) in
town; 90 km/h (55 mph)
on major roads (80 km/h
(50 mph)
in Switzerland); 130 km/h
(80 mph) on freeways
(120 km/h (75 mph) in
Switzerland)*
Car rental
Numerous agencies in
Milan and the airports.
The major companies
(Avis, Hertz, Europcar)
have branches in the
large towns (Varese,
Lugano, Como, Bergamo,
Brescia).

BY BIKE

Town centers
Como's *Città Murata* and
the center of Brescia are a
haven for cyclists.
Monte Isola (E D3)
→ *Bicycle rental on the
Peschiera lungolago*
Car-free island!
In Switzerland
Main roads with cycle
lanes.

Transportation around the Italian Lakes

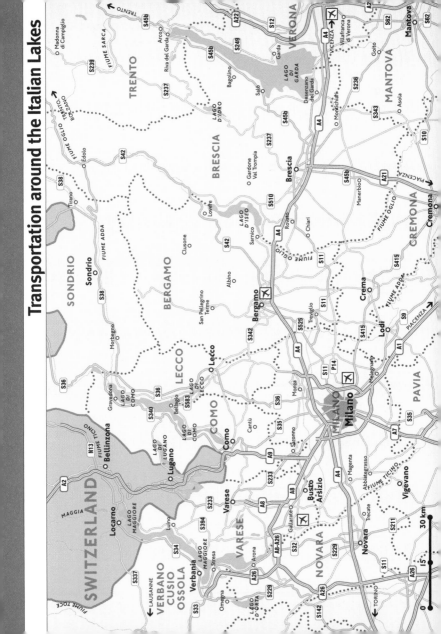

AIRPORTS

www.sea-aeroportimilano.it
Aeroporto E. Forlanini (Milan Linate)
→ 4.3 miles from Milan
European and national flights.
Aeroporto Intercont. della Malpensa (Milan)
→ Gallarate, 9 miles from Lake Maggiore. Bus links with Lake Maggiore (daily April-Oct) and Lugano International flights.
Bergamo
Orio al Serio (E B3)
Bus link with Brescia (daily)
www.orioaeroporto.it
European and national flights.

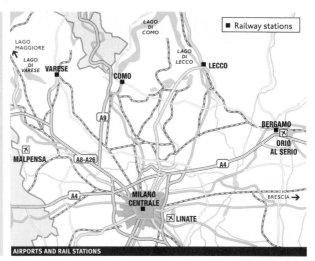

AIRPORTS AND RAIL STATIONS

■ Railway stations

Unless otherwise stated, prices shown are for a standard double room in high season with bathroom and breakfast (prima colazione). Prices tend to drop by about 30% in low season. Expect long annual closures, usually from the beginning of November to Easter, except in the big cities. Reservation is recommended in high season (July-Sep). Half-board and full board are available in most hotels. Farm breaks (agriturismo) usually have better facilities and represent better value for money than hotels (reservation essential). Beware: some hotels only accept bookings of a minimum of three nights. The Association of Historical Places of Italy is a non-profit organization which promotes shops, cafés and restaurants which were built at least 70 years

ago, and that have been and still are of cultural importance to the Italian nation. It is worth browsing its website (www.localistorici.it) as staying in one of the hotels listed there could be a treat.

A LAGO D'ORTA / GOLFO BORROMEO

Baveno (A C2)
La Ripa
→ Via Sempione, 11
Tel. 0323 924589 April-Dec
Crockery on the walls, red chairs and snug armchairs, the decor of this 11-room hotel is cozy and welcoming. Private beach. 62–85 €.

Mergozzo (A B1)
Le Oche di Bracchio
→ Via Bracchio, 46
Tel. 0322 80122
This hotel, surrounded by orchards, has 16 quiet, spacious rooms. The proprietor and chef, Italo

Malchioldi, holds improvised yoga lessons in the fields. From 94 €.

Stresa (A C3)
Grand Hôtel des îles Borromée
→ Corso Umberto I, 67
Tel. 0323 938938
With its monumental glass canopy over the entrance and chandeliers and gilding in the lobby, the Grand Hotel (1861) is popular with wealthy customers for its wide range of facilities (swimming pools, tennis courts, health spa etc.). 176 rooms; from 286 €.

Verbania Pallanza (A D2)
Albergo Villa Azalea
→ Salita S. Remigio, 4
Tel. 0323 556692 March-Oct
This magnificent villa (1930), tucked away in a quiet no-through road, is full of character, well-maintained and managed by Enrico Leccardi. You can enjoy breakfast in the

picturesque garden during the summer. 12 rooms, from 80 €.

Quarna Sopra (A A3)
Albergo Belvedere
→ Via Belvedere
Tel. 0323 826198 March-Dec
Perched at an altitude of 2,953 feet at the end of a long twisting road, the 'Belvedere' commands a breathtaking view of Lake Orta. 24 rooms, from 54 €.

B LAGO MAGGIORE

Brezzo di Bedero (B C3)
Agriturismo La Betulla
→ Via Belmonte, 7/9
Tel. 0332 532880 March-Nov
www.agriturismobetulla.it
Four wood-paneled apartments. The Zigliani family – cattle breeders – built their farm on a plateau beside a birch wood (betulla in Italian) with views of the lake. 350 € per week, without breakfast.

MONTE ISOLA

TOWARD MONTE GENEROSO

PORT DE TORRI DEL BENACO

Tel. 030 916078
www.hotelflaminia.com
A very pretty hotel, recently renovated and right on the lakefront. 85 rooms, from 110 €.

Castelnuovo del Garda (F C6)
Agriturismo Finilon
→ Loc. Finilon
Tel. 045 7572114
An 18th-century Venetian farm with courtyard and characteristic corner tower. Six simple rooms with large, comfy beds and large wardrobes. 40–45 €.

Garda (F C5)
Locanda San Vigilio
→ Punta San Vigilio
Tel. 045 7256688 Feb-Nov
www.gardalake.it/sanvigilio
On the picturesque site of Saint Vigil's Point, this hotel has seven luxurious rooms with a loggia, and three suites with private gardens featuring four-poster beds, original stone fireplace (16th century),

oriental rugs etc. 235–370 €.

Torri del Benaco (F C4)
Hotel Gardesana
→ Piazza Calderini, 20
Tel. 045 7225411 Feb-Nov
www.hotel-gardesana.com
The hotel is housed in the former harbormaster's office, built in 1452, with views of the old port and the Scaliger Castle. It has 34 comfortable standard rooms with Venetian motifs. Attractive arcade where you can enjoy a drink or bite to eat and one of the best restaurants on this side of the lake. 112–134 €.

Riva del Garda (B D1)
La Montanara
→ Via Montanara, 20
Tel. 0464 554857 April-Oct
This popular hotel, run by the friendly proprietor, Marisa, is located on one of Riva's colorful lanes. Nine quiet rooms with parquet floors. 43–46 €.

Gardone Riviera (F B4)
Grand Hotel Gardone
→ Via Zinardelli, 84
Tel. 0365 20261 April-Oct
www.grandgardone.it
An elegant tower is the landmark for the most prestigious hotel on Lake Garda (1886), founded by Viennese engineer, Ludwig Wimmer. Restaurant tables, swimming pool and garden on the long shorefront terrace. 180 rooms; from 185 €.

Salo (F B3)
Laurin
→ Viale Landi 9
Tel. 0365 22022
www.laurinsalo.com
One of the most enchanting places to stay by Lake Garda, this Art Nouveau-style villa was turned into a hotel fifty years ago. It has magnificent, stylish frescoed public rooms, a park, swimming pool and beach access. Gourmet restaurant too. From 125 €.

LAKE CRUISES

Boats run to the towns along the shore all year round.
→ Arona–Locarno (**B**) in 4hrs; Como–Colico (**D**) in 3 ½ hrs; Riva–Desenzano (**F**) in 4 ½ hrs

Transportation companies
Navigazione Laghi
→ Tel. 800 551801 (toll-free)
This national company is responsible for boat services on Lakes Maggiore, Como and Garda. Several high-speed hydroplane routes.

Società Navigazione Lago di Lugano
→ Tel. 091 923 1779
Operates a service on Lake Lugano.

Navigazione Lago d'Iseo
→ Tel. 035 971483
Operates a service on Lake Iseo.

Navigazione Lago d'Orta
→ Tel. 0322 844862
Operates a service on Lake Orta.

Night cruises
→ July-Aug: Fri-Sat
Tel. 800 551801 (toll-free)
Dinner dances on Lakes Maggiore and Como.

Renting a boat
→ Contact the companies direct for information

Bateau taxi
→ Prices negotiable
Cross by motoscafo (motorboat).

FERRIES

The three largest lakes (Maggiore, Como and Garda) operate a ferry service (routes shown on map above left)
→ Journey time: 15 to 30 mins

Street names, monuments and places to visit are listed alphabetically. They are followed by a map reference of which the initial letter in bold (**A**, **B**, **C**...) relates to the area and matching map.

NAVIGAZIONE LAGO MAGGIORE
ISOLE BORROMEE - ALL DESTINATIONS

LANDING STAGE AT STRESA

RESERVA NATURALE DI FONDO TOCE · S34 · Intra
GOLFO BORROMEO
Suna
Verbania
Pallanza
VILLA TARANTO
ISOLA MADRE
ISOLA S. GIOVANNI
Baveno
ISOLA SUPERIORE DEI PESCATORI
LAGO MAGGIORE
ISOLA BELLA
CARCIANO
Stresa
Levo

Optional route
Mandatory route
Landing stage

THE ISLANDS AND THE BORROMEO GULF

THE BORROMEO ISLANDS

Boats run to three of the four islands all year round: Bella, Pescatori, Madre (**A** C2–3). Single route with two request stops (Carciano and Villa Taranto), which do not operate in winter.
Information
Direzione Navigazione Lago Maggiore
→ *Tel. 800 551801 (toll-free)*
By vaporetto
→ *Daily, every 30 mins, 7am–7pm in summer; every 90 mins, 7am–6.30pm in winter. 1–6 € depending on journey*
By motoscafo
→ *Price negotiable*
Motorboats operating as water taxis.

D LAGO DI COMO

Bellagio (**D** B3)
La Pergola
→ *Piazza del Porto, 4*
Tel. 031 950263 March–Nov
www.lapergolabellagio.it
This quiet hotel can only be reached by a footpath through the fields. Leafy pergola above the old port, and interior decorated with antiques. From 100 €.
Carate Urio (**D** A5)
Albergo Ristorante Fioroni
→ *Piazza Minoletti, 1*
Tel. 031 400149 March–Nov
Each of the hotel's seven blue and white rooms has a breathtaking lake view. Restaurant terrace on the waterfront. From 77 €.
Cernobbio (**D** A5)
Villa d'Este
→ *Tel. 031 3481*
www.villadeste.it
The 'villa of delight' was built by Pellegrino Tibaldi (1570). Luxurious rooms and a superb garden dotted with

waterfalls. Floating swimming pool on the lake. A dream. From 600 €.
Consiglio Rumo (**D** C1)
Agriturismo La Sorgente
→ *Loc. Brenzio, 24*
Tel. 0344 81859 April–Oct
In a remote mountainside hamlet in Gravedona, the 'Spring' has two apartments decorated with local furniture by Signora Ciappa. Breakfast on large tables. Excellent homemade jams. 250 € per week.

E BERGAMO / LAGO D'ISEO / BRESCIA

Bergamo (**E** C1)
Il Sole
→ *Via B. Colleoni, 1*
Tel. 035 218238
Opened in 1873, this hotel couldn't be more central. Its ten rooms overlook the Piazza Vecchia in the Upper City. From 91 €.
San Vigilio
→ *Via San Vigilio, 15*

Tel. 035 253 179
www.sanvigilio.it
A great place to stay, high up on the hill beyond the *città alta*, with only seven rooms – five of which with magnificent views over the valley. Terrace and restaurant. From 95 €.
Alzano Lombardo (**E** B3)
Agriturismo Ardizzone
→ *Loc. Nese Tel. 035 510060*
At the mouth of the Seriana valley, five apartments giving onto the courtyard of a large 15th-century farm. Horse-riding and archery. From 58 €.
Monte Isola (**E** D3)
La Foresta
→ *Loc. Peschiera Maraglio*
Tel. 030 9886210 March–Oct
On the island of Monte Isola, surrounded by olive trees, the 'Forest' hotel is run by the entire Novali family: Signor Novali drives the water taxi, Signora Novali cooks and their children work in the hotel.

Small pontoon for sun-worshippers. Ten rooms. From 73 €.
Scanzorosciate (**E** B3)
Agriturismo Donecco
→ *Via Serradesca, 9*
Tel. 035 4599639
Two quiet apartments with all mod cons in a huge farm at the bottom of a small valley with vine-covered slopes. From 80 €.

F LAGO DI GARDA

Sirmione (**F** B5)
Villa Paradiso
→ *Via Arici, 7*
Tel. 030 916149 April–Oct
The 'Paradise' villa, at the tip of the peninsula, is truly deserving of its name. Garden planted with orange trees, walnuts and cypresses and hotel run by the Sordelli sisters furnished with family heirlooms (six rooms). From 75 €.
Flaminia
→ *Piazza Flaminia, 8*